D0466875

BERING BRIDGE

The Soviet-American Expedition from Siberia to Alaska

Co-leaders Dmitry Shparo (left) and Paul Schurke envisioned an adventure that would rebuild an ancient bridge between cultures.

BERING BRIDGE

The Soviet-American Expedition from Siberia to Alaska

PAUL SCHURKE

Pfeifer-Hamilton

Pfeifer-Hamilton, Publisher 1702 E Jefferson St
Duluth MN 55812 (218) 728-6807

BERING BRIDGE

The Soviet-American Expedition from Siberia to Alaska

Printed in the United States of America by Worzalla Publishing.

10 9 8 7 6 5 4 3 2 1

Book design by Riechmann Pederson Design Inc., Minneapolis MN
Illustrations by Peter Gross
Library of Congress Cataloging in Publication Data
89-063089

ISBN 0-938586-31-9

Photographs by the author except where noted.
Front jacket flap, upper left: photo by Michio Hoshino, courtesy of Alaska Airlines.
Facing title page: photo courtesy of Novosti press agency.

For Bria and Samuel

To the Members of the Bering Bridge Expedition:

I am greeting you with all my heart, you the members of
the Soviet-American expedition with the name "The Bering
Bridge."

The name is not just a symbol for me. This name
represents my own true feelings. You are truly helping to
build a bridge of friendship and cooperation between
Chukotka and Alaska as well as between the Soviet Union
and the United States. We are united by common
challenges such as preserving northern cultures, protecting
the arctic ecosystem and, of course, the most important
challenge, the strengthening of peaceful relations among all
countries of the world.

I wish you the best of luck, great success and may all your
goals be accomplished.

Mikhail Gorbachev

General Secretary, U.S.S.R.
April 21, 1989

Greetings to the members of the Bering Bridge Expedition
as you complete your trek from Anadyr, Siberia to
Kotzebue, Alaska.

Crossing more than 1,000 miles and the treacherous waters
of the Bering Strait, your journey has been a remarkable
demonstration of human strength and stamina. But more
important, it has reminded us of the close ties which unite
the Eskimo peoples on both sides of the Strait. You can be
proud of your role in helping to strengthen those ties.

In their official orders dated January 2, 1719, the Russian
explorers Fedor Luzhin and Ivan Evreinov were told to
answer the question: "Are America and Asia joined?"
Thanks to your efforts, this 270-year old question can be
answered, "yes."

Congratulations to you all on this fine accomplishment.
May the future bring each of you continued success and
every happiness, and may God bless you always.

George Bush

President, USA
May 8, 1989

Twelve people from diverse backgrounds shared a common goal.

ACKNOWLEDGMENTS

My first thanks must go to my team members. They had as little idea as I did about what to expect from this ambitious scheme when they agreed to take part. But they handled their dual roles as adventurers and citizen diplomats with commitment and aplomb.

I will be forever grateful to them—Dmitry, Sasha, Alexander, Zoya, Vadim, Cola, Lonnie, Ginna, Ernie, Robert and Darlene—for sharing this odyssey with me.

I am also grateful to the thousands of Soviet and American villagers who endorsed our vision with their outpourings of warmth and generosity during our visits to their communities: Anadyr, Uelkal, Egvikinot, Konergino, Enmelen, Nunligran, Sireniki, Provideniya, New Chaplino, Yanrakinot, Lorino, Lavrentiya, Uelen, Ratmanova, Litte Diomede, Wales, Brevig Mission, Teller, Nome and Kotzebue.

Many people nurtured the Bering Bridge Expedition when it was just the spark of an idea. Among those for whom I feel deep gratitude for helping me fan the spark into flames are Rick and Amy Donahue, Phil Kugzruk, Anne Walker, Dr. Ted Mala and Mary Core.

Others fueled the fire with their ready offers of sponsorship assistance. For this, I am grateful first and foremost to our friends at Du Pont Thermax, including Jeff McGuire and Duane Roach and their communications representative Jeff Blumenfeld for providing the bulk of our financial needs and for hiring Anne Walker to serve as our communications coordinator.

To the management team at Alaska Airlines, including Bruce Kennedy, Jim Johnson and Doug Versteeg, I am very thankful not only for all the air transport services they arranged for us but also for the insights I gained about teamwork while observing them respond to difficult situations.

Many thanks also go to our other key Alaskan sponsors, Ron Sheardown of Greatland Exploration, Lee Wareham of Alascom and Jim Rowe of Bering Air, who were sources of material assistance and sage advice.

I also want to acknowledge with gratitude our Soviet sponsors, which included the youth newspaper Komsomolskaya Pravda, the national travel organzation Sputnik and the news agency Novosti.

Many American companies provided equipment or supplies. Among these are Hills Pet Products, R.E.I, Fischer Ski of America, Red Wing Shoe Company, S. B. Foot Tanning Company, Shaklee Corporation, Servus Rubber Company, Surefoot Company, Brunton Compasses and Fox River Mills.

Many government officials shared the vision that the Bering Bridge Expedition could enhance Soviet-American relations.

Among those on the American side who stood by us to make sure that bureaucracy did not stand in the way are Wayne Neill of the U.S. State Department, Alaskan Governor Steve Cowper and his staff, including David Ramseur and Robert Poe, and U.S. Senator from Alaska Frank Murkowski and his staff, including Jessica Gavora. On the Soviet side these included Governor Vyacheslav Kobetz, Nicolai Kashtikin and Nahdezhda Ohtke.

Gratitude also goes to many individuals who believed in us and volunteered their talents and labor. These included our kennel manager Dean Amsbaugh, veterinarian Gretchen Gerber, dog handler Tom Conaway, my brother John Schurke, Sue Steineker and Mary Lykum.

My publisher Don Tubesing, a creative and committed citizen diplomat, was a wellspring of enthusiasm for this project. His company, Pfeifer-Hamilton Publishers, became one of our financial sponsors and he was a steadfast source of encouragement and support before, during and after the trek. He and master wordsmith Larry Fortner buoyed me along as I struggled to put this story on *paper before my mukluks even had time to dry. Susan Gustafson also contributed mightily by transcribing hours of tapes and by watching over the preparation of the text of this book with a caring eye.*

Finally, and most important, heaps of thanks and hugs and kisses go to my wife, pal and business partner, Susan Hendrickson, for covering my parenting duties, carrying our second child, maintaining our home, paying the bills, shoveling the driveway, feeding our puppies and praying for me while I was gone. She helped keep me warm not only with her thoughts but with her handiwork as well. She and her staff at Wintergreen Designs—Deb Erdman, Eileen Frisell, Susan Meisner—designed and produced in a few weeks time some 750 items of clothing and equipment that served our team flawlessly throughout our journey.

Paul Schurke
Ely, Minnesota

Wind-whipped snow enveloped the team in a world of white.

Skiing through the pale arctic daylight, I searched the Siberian tundra for a touch of color, a detail, even a shadow, but the sky merged with the ground and enveloped me and my teammates in a world of white.

We hadn't detected so much as a hint of the native village we were headed for.

We had been slogging our way on skis and dog sleds for a full week through whiteouts and wind storms, and we were weary. We would welcome a warm meal and refuge from the punishing elements in this region so justly known as the "birthplace of blizzards."

The Eskimo settlement we were approaching was on the Soviet coast of the Bering Sea. The villagers had been alerted to our arrival and, on this day in late March 1989, they awaited their first visitors from the Western world in nearly half a century.

We numbered twelve—six Soviets and six Americans. We came from five cultures, and we spoke as many languages. Our nine men and three women included representatives of three arctic peoples—Yupik Eskimo, Inupiaq Eskimo and a Siberian people known as Chukchi. Also in our group were Americans from Alaska and Minnesota, and Soviets from Moscow.

Our expedition was taking us on a two-month trek across

the little-known Soviet state of Chukotka, across the treacherous waters of the Bering Strait and onto the western tip of Alaska. Our mission was to improve relations between our countries.

We had set out to link the settlements that form a chain of habitation along the Soviet and American coasts. We were determined to encourage our countries to reopen the border and restore free travel by the native people on both sides of the Strait.

We were traversing the most remote reaches of the superpowers. The land we were crossing was nearly a quarter of the world away from their respective capitals. Nearly a thousand miles of ice, snow and ocean would pass beneath our skis and sled runners.

More important than the distance, though, were the stops we would make along the way. One of those stops was the settlement of reindeer herders and walrus hunters that we were approaching through the arctic whiteness this March evening.

As we crested a barely perceptible rise, the shapeless vista was finally broken by the faint trace of roof lines above homes nearly buried in the snow. From a half-mile distant I could see figures walking about.

We raised the flags of our two countries. The villagers noticed us, and suddenly the air was electric. People poured from their homes. Our dogs bounded forward.

Children raced toward our team, waving handmade paper American flags. A volley of green fireworks showered overhead. Drawing closer, we could see a huge red banner stretched across the front of the crowd. "Welcome dear friends!" it said in English and Russian.

The heavy, pulsing rhythm of skin drums filled the air. Young dancers wearing beaded headdresses and garments of wolverine, reindeer and seal gestured gracefully with their hands as a chorus was half sung and half chanted by their elders behind them. *K'eye yah'ag, k'eye yah'ag, k'eye ya,* they sang in the soft guttural clucking sounds of Yupik, a language shared by two of our team members—Zoya, a Soviet Eskimo, and Darlene, an American Eskimo.

The crowd swallowed us up in bear hugs of welcome.

For the villagers, our arrival was proof positive that the

winds of change are sweeping even the most remote corners of our world. For the past few decades an Ice Curtain between the United States and the Soviet Union had separated native communities that once knew no international borders. Our being in the village signaled our desire to lift that Ice Curtain.

The Bering Bridge Expedition was highly ambitious and idealistic, but was it realistic?

Could our team, a hastily gathered collection of men and women with various levels of expedition experience, overcome the harsh conditions of the Siberian winter? Could we safely cross the Bering Strait?

What tensions would result from struggling to communicate in five languages?

Could we actually bring two nations together at the International Date Line?

How would our vision take shape? What would emerge from the dream as we lived it?

Our journey would answer those questions.

For elders of two nations—cultures reconnnected.

For a child of Chukotka—a bridge reopened.

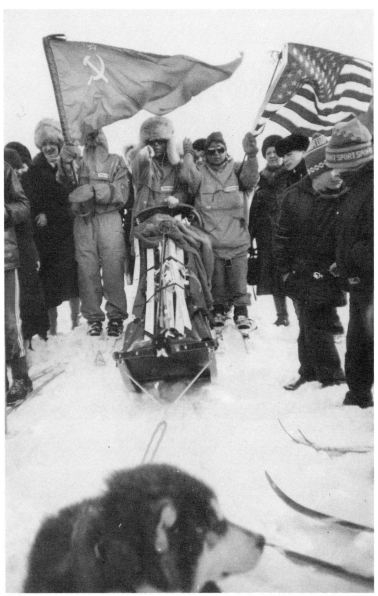

With flags unfurled, the "dog sled diplomats" entered the native villages.

ONE

ОДИН

The string of events that led me to the Bering Bridge Expedition began two years earlier and 2,000 miles away. I was standing at the North Pole.

I had reached the pole by dog team with five companions at the dramatic conclusion of the Steger International Polar Expedition. Will Steger and I had assembled a team of seven men and one woman from the U.S., Canada and New Zealand; raised a half million dollars; trained 50 freight dogs; and, with the help of my wife, Susan Hendrickson, produced the clothing and equipment we needed.

On May 1, 1986, we became the first people in recorded history to reach the pole without resupply. Triumphantly posing arm-in-arm behind a blue banner on which was emblazoned a single word — *Peace*—we read a short statement for the journalists who had been flown up for the occasion.

"Standing here, where the lines of longitude of all countries meet," our message concluded, "we dedicate this journey to the hope that other seemingly impossible goals might be met by people everywhere."

For months following the North Pole journey we were swept along in a blur of press events, public appearances and speaking tours. The accolades were extremely gratifying to me, and so was the new identity of "world-class polar explorer" that came with it. The identity didn't wear well, though, because it wasn't me. My adventure experiences have been defined more by the people I'm with than by the wilderness I'm in. For me the value of wilderness challenges is in their ability to change people.

Starting from that moment at the North Pole, I had a deep yearning that my next adventure would not take me through uninhabited polar wastes; I sought a journey that would allow me to apply in a real and tangible way that word—*Peace*—that we had flown at the Pole.

The most effective way that could be done, I believed, was through an expedition that would link people of the two super-powers in a meaningful gesture of peace.

I knew that one place to complete such a trek between the U.S. and the Soviet Union was at the Bering Strait.

Out there in the Strait is an imaginary line. This invisible boundary ranks among the world's most significant features. It is the International Date Line. This global seam separates today from tomorrow, the Americas from Eurasia, the United States from the Soviet Union.

In the Bering Strait, between the islands of Soviet Big Diomede and American Little Diomede, only two and a half miles of ocean separate the two countries. The Date Line runs exactly between them. Only a little more than 50 miles of water separate the mainlands. The U.S. and the Soviet Union are each other's nearest overseas neighbors.

In our distant past, the great glaciers of the Ice Age absorbed so much water that ocean levels dropped hundreds of feet, exposing a land bridge from Siberia to Alaska.

It's likely that the people who ventured into this area from central Asia 16,000 years ago placed the first human footprints on the soil of North America. The causeway later narrowed and flooded as the climate changed and the great glaciers melted.

The Eskimo elders in the village on Little Diomede tell tales of an ancient time when their people all lived on a sandbar that stretched between Big and Little Diomede. When the water rose, the people in that ancient time moved to the mile-wide dome of rock from where they still hunt today in skin boats for walruses, seals and beluga whales.

The treeless, windswept lands of the Bering Strait were

among the last to be charted by Western explorers and cartographers. Well into the 18th century the area remained a great blank on world maps, less known to outsiders than the heart of Africa.

The maritime Eskimos and the reindeer-herding Chukchi people had virtually no contact with the outside. They traveled freely by water or ice between the continents to trade and hunt, and sometimes pillage, and at other times to share dances and songs.

In the mid-1800s, although the flag of the czars was removed from Alaska and replaced by the Stars and Stripes, the Eskimos continued to stalk their migratory prey. They remained indifferent to the new border, but they did have a joke about the factitious Date Line. "We go hunting today," goes an adage of the Little Diomeders. "We kill tomorrow. And we butcher and eat it yesterday."

Even after the Russian Revolution reached the Siberian Far East in the early 1920s, Eskimo relatives on both sides maintained their old intimate ties. No one fussed over identification papers, paper currency or other tokens of sovereignty. Many Eskimo elders on both sides still clearly remember the era of open travel.

The first restrictions were imposed in 1938. The two powers agreed to allow visits by American Eskimos to continue as long as they registered with officials in the Soviet Union, stayed less than three months and brought no guns, whiskey or forbidden objects of religious worship. The agreement, which did not include reciprocal visits by Chukotkans, also regulated trade in fur and other materials.

With the outbreak of World War II, the Allies' need to supply the western front with lend-lease military equipment from American factories by the back door of Asia briefly accelerated the flow of traffic across the Bering Strait. That surge was only temporary. A few years after the Soviets flew the last of some 7,000 aircraft from Nome, Alaska, into their homeland, the door slammed shut behind them.

Ten years after the visitation agreement was signed, it fell victim to the Cold War. In May 1948 the Soviets informed the U.S. State Department that passage rights by natives had been terminated. In turn, the U.S. closed Alaska to visits by Chukot-kans.

This timeless crossroads of continents had been blocked with merely a stroke of a pen. The Bering Bridge was closed.

As I continued to learn about the Bering Strait region, the vision of the expedition was becoming clearer to me. I dreamed of a trek by dog sled and ski across the Strait. I was determined to play a role in reopening that ancient bridge.

By the spring of 1987 I was making plans in earnest. As the vision grew clearer, the plan called for a route that would connect as many communities on both sides of the Strait as possible. I also wanted a team that would reflect the diversity of people living in the Bering region—Soviets and Americans, natives and non-natives, men and women. Thus the team would be large: six from each country, with at least half being natives.

Unlike the North Pole journey, with all its fanfare and media attention to daring exploits and harrowing escapes, this Bering Bridge Expedition was to be built on soul rather than sensation.

Ordinary people were influencing relations between the U.S. and Soviet Union through school exchanges, cooperative business ventures and art programs. I wondered how I too could play a role.

The Bering Bridge Expedition was the answer.

I hadn't contacted the Soviets yet. I didn't even know how I would approach the Kremlin for approval. I had never been to Russia, and I didn't speak a word of the language. I just knew that if I had faith in the idea and was willing to pour my energy into it, it would happen. That was a lesson I'd gained from the polar trek.

I knew that my chances for approval from Moscow would be better if I had a detailed proposal. I focused first on the route, gathering maps from wherever I could.

Planning the trip along the Alaskan coast was easy. State and local officials were cooperative and enthusiastic.

Planning a crossing of the Bering Strait wasn't so easy. I learned that crossing the treacherous Strait in winter, with its stiff winds, strong currents and floating ice packs, was an iffy proposition. I also learned that weather and ocean currents are most stable in late March and early April. I planned our itinerary accordingly.

Selecting a route for the Soviet sector of the journey was even more difficult. I pooled all the maps I could find in public libraries. No two maps showed the same number and placement of villages along the coast of Chukotka. Some maps were radically different. One knowledgeable person suggested that the inconsistencies might have resulted from a cartographers' "shell game." In decades past, Soviet map makers were suspected of intentionally mislabeling strategic stretches of their coastlines to keep foreign military strategists guessing.

How could I make a solid proposal to Moscow without knowing the specifics of my route? That solution came courtesy of satellite reconnaissance. The World Aeronautical Chart of the Bering Region, issued by the U.S. National Oceanic and Atmospheric Administration as a navigation aid for pilots, accurately illustrates the topography of Chukotka. There on the chart I found that a string of settlements exists in neat succession along the entire south and east coastlines of the Chukotka peninsula.

As I studied the map the pieces of the trip for the Bering Bridge Expedition began to fall into place: Some 650 miles of overland travel would take us through 14 cities and villages in Chukotka. A 40-mile crossing of the Strait and a visit to the Soviet border patrol station on Big Diomede Island would complete the Soviet leg. Then we'd step two and a half miles across the International Date Line to Little Diomede. Next would come the 25-mile jump to Alaska. Finally we'd cap our journey with visits to another 12 communities on the U.S. coast.

I was convinced that this was an adventure just waiting to happen. The region was ready for an expedition that would set an example of Soviet-American cooperation and reconnect the cultures of eastern Chukotka and western Alaska.

I had started with a dream, and now I had a plan and a route. What I needed next was the go-ahead—and help.

No Americans had been granted Soviet permission to visit these Chukotkan communities since the border was closed in 1948—at least not when I began planning our expedition. While I laid the groundwork for this journey, other citizen diplomats were making plans with similar goals. In Alaska, for example, several initiatives for contacts with Chukotkans had been taken and were being viewed positively in the Soviet Union. From my perspective in Minnesota these initiatives hinted that the Soviets would be willing to open Chukotka to the Bering Bridge Expedition.

I pursued that approval by knocking on every door I could find. I attended international conferences; I spoke with corporate sponsors and medical researchers, international peace groups and Alaskan officials and entrepreneurs; and I tracked down Soviet adventurers and government officials wherever I could find them.

The breakthrough came in April 1988 with a phone call from Ottawa. It was Dmitry Shparo. Would I meet him in Toronto in two days to tell him more about my plan?

I was honored by his interest and leaped at the chance. Dmitry, a 47-year-old Muscovite, ranks as one of the foremost arctic adventurers in the world. Though little news of his accomplishments has appeared in the American press, he has led more polar expeditions than anyone alive. Twice he has reached the North Pole on skis.

Our first meeting in Canada was cordial, but he was something less than enthusiastic. He liked the concept of the Bering Bridge Expedition but was skeptical of my plans to include Eskimos and women. He doubted that they would have the training and experience to undertake such a long trek. I was certain that appropriate people could be found. Ann Bancroft had broken precedent as a member of our North Pole trek. She was the first woman to be part of a major arctic expedition.

Despite his initial reservations, Dmitry offered to circulate my written proposal among Soviet authorities. In the weeks that followed, Dmitry became much more enthusiastic. In July he summoned me to Canada again. The plan had been well received among Soviet authorities, and he had decided to join me as co-leader. He even thought it was possible to secure all necessary permissions to launch the trek the very next winter—not the year after, as I had planned.

I was astonished. An immediate launch would mean putting together a major expedition in six months—not the 18 to 24

DMITRY
Bearing red carnations

months that a project of such magnitude called for. Not only were the pieces falling in place—but they were falling all around me and all at once.

Despite Dmitry's confidence, I dismissed his notion of pulling a major expedition together in a few months' time. A training journey in Alaska or Siberia would be needed first. Furthermore, I was skeptical that Soviet authorities would so quickly approve our plan to traverse one of the most tightly secured and militarily strategic regions of their country. Even Soviet citizens need special visas to enter Chukotka.

Nonetheless Dmitry and I agreed to the basic terms of the project. Our 12-member team would be made up of equal numbers of Soviets and Americans as well as natives and non-natives. Dmitry also agreed to include women. We arranged to meet again in the fall in Moscow.

In the meantime I traveled to Alaska to plan the expedition's visits to villages there. I also waited to hear again from Dmitry.

In mid-October he sent me a telex. Soviet authorities had granted approval for us to travel to Chukotka to discuss our plan. I was issued a visa to visit the Soviet Union for two weeks in November. Final permission for the expedition was still pending, Dmitry said, but things looked good. We were on a roll.

I could hardly contain my excitement when my British Airways flight touched down at Shermetevo Airport on a snowy November day. I was in Moscow! And it had all happened so fast!

Dmitry, this rugged polar explorer, greeted me in the terminal with a handful of red carnations. So much for the popular image of the cold and stoic Soviet.

For the next few days we raced around Moscow for meetings with sponsors. Then came a nine-hour flight—more than 6,000 miles—to the far northeastern corner of Dmitry's vast country. We were in Chukotka—beyond Siberia, at the far tip of the Soviet Union. There in the remote land that had fired my imagination, we had two more days of meetings, and officials there gave Dmitry and me a firm stamp of approval.

Furthermore, they urged doing the trip in the coming winter. "One never knows what next year will bring," said one government official. That only made me nervous. I still wondered how we would pull the project together so quickly.

While we were in Chukotka, we proposed that the port city of Anadyr be the starting point for our trek and the location of our communications base for the Soviet segment of our expedition. Once again, our proposal was soundly endorsed by local officials.

During that trip, we were also able to get to Lorino, a small native settlement along the Soviet coast of the Bering Strait. There we were received by a dozen Eskimo elders at a feast they had prepared for us in the community hall. Their faces looked exactly like those I had seen months earlier in my planning visits in Alaska. Much of the food was the same as well—salmon, reindeer, seal and *muktuk*—cubes of skin from the beluga whale. Also served were bowls of Russian chocolate and black bread. Tea was served from a samovar, an ornate metal urn. Our hosts wore conventional Russian clothing but on their feet wore Eskimo boots of beaded sealskin and caribou.

For the first time I was seeing the assimilation—or jarring juxtaposition—of cultures. The next months would be rich with more examples.

Among themselves, the natives of Lorino spoke Yupik. To Dmitry, they spoke Russian, a language I was just beginning to learn.

Through Dmitry, I told the Chukotkan natives that Alaskan Eskimos wanted to reestablish cultural contacts. Did the natives in Chukotka feel the same? I asked. The answer came passionately, translated from Yupik to Russian to English: They were "burning" to renew those ancient ties. They dearly remembered the days when boatloads of Alaskan Eskimos would arrive each summer for their annual festival of games, song and dance. Oh, how they would love to relive those days.

They were excited about our plan and offered to help Dmitry find native team members and sled dogs. I was deeply moved. I understood now more than ever how significant our expedition could be.

After returning to Moscow, Dmitry and I spent a few more days together in frantic planning. He too had been moved by the enthusiasm for our project throughout Chukotka and was more determined than ever to launch the trip that winter. "Why wait?" he said to me. "The people of Chukotka are now counting on us."

Dmitry also said that he had received formal authorization for our plan from the Soviet government.

This trip was going to fly—and it was cleared for immediate takeoff.

My head was spinning as I returned to my home in Minnesota. The next two months were a blur of planning and resource-gathering. My wife, Susan, produced the clothing. Key sponsors signed on. I assembled five other American team members. Three were Eskimos from Alaska's Bering region: Robert Soolook, 23, a National Guardsman from Little Diomede Island; Darlene Apangalook, 25, a college student from Gambell; and Ernie Norton, 45, a salmon fisherman from Kotzebue. The other two were Ginna Brelsford, 30, an international trade specialist in Anchorage for the office of the governor of Alaska; and Lonnie Dupre, 27, a carpenter from Coon Rapids, Minnesota.

On March 1, 1989, we were on our way to Anadyr in Chukotka. The journey of the Bering Bridge Expedition was about to begin.

The collective in Anadyr made beautiful skin clothing for the team.

Ancient traditions greeted the modern adventurers.

TWO

ДВА

"We go to Siberia!" chirped my three-year-old, Bria, as she marched up and down the aisle of the Boeing 737 that we had chartered to take our team from Anchorage to Anadyr. Bria, Susan and nearly 50 other passengers, including journalists and business officials, were accompanying us to our send-off in Anadyr.

Bria's joyful enthusiasm was contagious. All of us were swept up in child-like excitement. In less than two hours we would reach the land that once had seemed a world away.

A half hour into our flight, the pilot announced, "We've just crossed the International Date Line. Welcome to tomorrow." That brought a burst of cheers from the passengers.

I adjusted my watch. Given the date change and a jog in time zones, we had jumped 21 hours ahead of Alaska time. From noon on Wednesday, March 1, to 9:00 a.m. on Thursday, March 2, in a fleeting moment.

"This is great," joked one of the journalists. "When I get back home from Anadyr, I will for once be able to file an accurate story about tomorrow's weather."

Below us we could see only the white expanse of Bering Sea ice. Then suddenly the Soviet mainland came into view. My teammates and I glued our faces to the windows to catch a glimpse of the rugged hills and mountains that line the frozen coastline we would soon be traveling by dog sled.

When we spotted villages below us we marveled at these isolated islands of life. These 14 communities were the focus of our project. No highways stretch between them. They are accessible only by air, water or tough, all-terrain vehicles. Some of the villages are only a few dozen miles apart. Others are separated by more than a hundred miles.

Those miles passed under us in what seemed a wink of time, and, when we reached the base of the Chukotka Peninsula, the pilot announced our descent into Anadyr—this city of 12,000—the capital of Chukotka. The pilots reported that it was minus 10 degrees outside with a wind chill of minus 35.

As we filed down the ramp we were greeted by a sea of wide-eyed faces. I searched for a familiar face and found Dmitry beaming at me through a mantle of fur and frost. "Welcome, dear Paul!" he shouted over the roar of the wind. We embraced like old friends, and he beckoned me toward an opening in the crowd.

Two radiant young women, strikingly costumed in native fur garments with beaded headpieces and bright floral shawls, offered us a sculpted loaf of brown bread and a basin of salt.

"A Great Russian tradition. Please take a little bread with salt and eat," Dmitry instructed me.

Then Alexander Tenyakshev, 42, and Sasha Belayev, 30, greeted us. I had met them in November in Moscow. Alexander, a communications professor, would serve as our radio operator. Sasha, a research engineer with much expedition experience, would be in charge of our rations. Both of them spoke English. Our team was nine.

"Our Chukotkan team members await us in town," said Alexander as I glanced around, looking for the three additional Soviet teammates.

The airport scene was hectic. A few hundred people were standing on the runway to greet us. Eighty or so of the people were military officers who had been assigned to escort us. Five yellow school buses and 20 jeeps ringed the plane to take us to the nearest building—a mile away. Fifty reporters, Soviet and Western, were scrambling to record the scene before all the participants froze.

Finally, interpreters moved through the crowds, urging, "To

the bus. Please, everyone, to the bus now." With the wind ripping at our clothes and freezing our cameras, we climbed into jeeps and buses.

In town, Dmitry escorted us into a side room of the community auditorium and presented us to three more people. "Our three new friends from Chukotka," he said proudly.

One of them, Vadim Krivolap, I recognized. I had met him during my November visit. Vadim is a tall strapping sportsman. He peered out at me from under his mop of curly black hair with a shy smile. "Very good to see you, Paul," he said, surprising me with his newly learned English.

Next to him stood a short muscular man with black hair and strong native features that almost looked Oriental. This was Nicolai Attinya, or, as we knew him throughout our journey— Cola.

Cola and Vadim were our Chukchi team members. Best friends since childhood and both 25 years old, they are residents of Neshkan, a 900-member community on the Chukotka Peninsula's north coast. Vadim serves as youth program director for the village's Young Communist League. Cola is the school's wrestling coach. Through competitions nationwide, Cola had achieved the rank of Master Sportsman, one of the highest honors bestowed upon Russian athletes. Both men spend their spare time as hunters, reindeer herders and dog mushers. Cola had brought 11 dogs with him. They would be used in two teams. Cola knew only a few words of English, but that would change rapidly in the weeks to come.

Our third Soviet native teammate was an Eskimo woman with distinctive high cheek bones, sparkling dark eyes and a bright smile. Her hair was neatly coiffed, and she was wearing a brown skirt and tan blouse. "You must be Zoya Ivanova," I said, embracing her.

"Yes, me Zoya," she said with the cheery laugh that would become her trademark on the trail. Dmitry had informed me earlier about this remarkable 42-year-old Yupik Eskimo woman. A pediatrician, mother of four and one of the lead dancers with the Eskimo dance company in her village of Lavrentiya, she would serve as our team doctor and drive one of Cola's dog teams.

I hoped she would be strong enough for the journey. Dmitry had privately expressed similar concerns to me.

"Please now we must hurry to the program," Dmitry said as he ushered us out. In the arrangement between the U.S. State Department and the Soviet Ministry of Aviation, our plane's landing rights had been granted for only six hours.

On our way to the auditorium, I was introduced to our interpreter, Natasha, who would work with us during our stay in Anadyr. Natasha is a high school English teacher. Soviet education policy calls for providing all school children with at least two years of instruction in English. Natasha spoke with a crisp Oxford cadence.

Once in the auditorium, we assembled on a stage and nervously waved back to the cheering crowd that included our American entourage and as many residents of Anadyr as could squeeze into the room. When the national anthems of both countries were played and the flags were saluted, my eyes welled with tears of pride for this project.

I choked out the few Russian words of greeting I knew, and then with Natasha's help I told the crowd that this was one of the proudest moments of my life.

"The journey we are about to embark on is not so much one of adventure but rather one of hope," I said. "We hope it nurtures the growing friendship between Alaska and Chukotka, the U.S. and the Soviet Union."

A banquet followed, and then the Americans who had accompanied us had to gather in the city's square to await rides back to the airport. In the final electric moments of this cross-cultural rendezvous, the spirit of fellowship and goodwill built to a crescendo—for Soviets and Americans alike. Everyone hurriedly exchanged gifts and addresses. The American journalists cornered every English-speaking Soviet they could find for last-minute interviews.

One Soviet woman, in tears, tugged at a reporter's jacket, desperate to have him understand her Russian comments. Finally an interpreter was found. "I never thought I would live to see the day when Americans would land in peace in our town," were the words she wanted to share with the reporter. She pointed toward a huge banner stretched across a building. The banner proclaimed in English, "The Bering Bridge Is the Bridge of Friendship between Soviet and American People."

Susan, Bria and I caught a ride to the airport ahead of the others to enjoy a few final moments together. Susan was two months pregnant, and she would return to our wilderness home in Ely, Minnesota, to manage her business. She would keep up to date with our progress by talking with Anne Walker, our base operator in Nome. Many weeks would pass before Susan and I would be able to talk with each other again.

Our first full day in Anadyr, Thursday, March 3, broke clear, cold and calm. From the narrow window of my tiny hotel room, I watched a tangerine sun rise and send its light through the fog. "Americans and Siberians share the same light," I thought as I gazed homeward. Just such thoughts would help keep homesickness at bay throughout the long journey ahead.

Over breakfast I asked Dmitry, "What day do you think our expedition can depart?" Our team was seated around a long linen-covered table in the hotel's tidy little restaurant, eating dark bread and cold sausage with cheese.

"I don't know," he said. "Maybe this weekend. But we have much to do." He was harried. He had an endless string of logistical details to attend to with local officials. The Soviet team—together with a four-person support crew from Moscow—had arrived here just a couple of days before we had. I had hoped that our first day would open with a thorough team discussion about our plans and goals. Dmitry had shrugged at that suggestion. Meetings, I would find, were anathema to him. "All people can get to know each other without big meeting," he said.

Communication obstacles, of course, would make that difficult. But everyone was making an effort to get acquainted, and alliances already were starting to form.

Zoya and Darlene, who were sharing a hotel room, had hit it off as instant friends. No language barrier stood between them. They spoke similar dialects of Yupik. The bridge was forming already.

A friendship was also developing between Ginna and Sasha. They had decided to share the responsibility of looking after the expedition rations, which had been provided by the Soviet team.

Lonnie had teamed up with Cola and Vadim the night before to look after our sled dogs. When I asked how they were communicating, he said, "Lots of pantomime and lots of laughs."

In the morning we gave blood samples and subjected ourselves to fitness tests for Soviet medical researchers who were doing a study on cold weather physiology in conjunction with our expedition. We also received from them a diary filled with questionnaires regarding our moods. We were to fill out one of the questionnaires each day.

In the evening we took part in a press conference aired live over local television. The TV session went well, but led to a change in our plans. "The news has made a mistake," Dmitry informed me later that night. "It tells all people that expedition leaves tomorrow. Now people in Anadyr have plans to come to the square and say goodbye to us. What can we do?" he asked.

"Let's have a parade!" I said. "We can run the dog teams down the street and no one will be disappointed."

He liked it. The plan was set. But like other staged events on this trek, the parade wouldn't go quite as we hoped.

After lunch on Saturday, Cola, Vadim, Lonnie and Robert harnessed up our two American and two Soviet dog teams and brought them to the front of the hotel. Many of us put on sets of native skin clothing that had been presented to us the day before by the town's sewing collective.

Vadim and Cola were dressed head to toe in native costume, with sealskin mukluks and bonnet-style caribou hats with wolverine trim. They were absolutely stunning. It was hard to believe these were the same guys who had been running around in jeans and sweat shirts that morning. In their traditional clothing, they were back in their element—they're accustomed to wearing skin clothing while herding reindeer on the tundra back home.

The parade proved to be highly popular. Before we had the sleds ready to go, the streets were jammed with thousands of townspeople. Many of them had been at work the day we arrived and they hadn't yet had a chance to get their first view of the

LONNIE
Pantomime and laughter

American visitors. "This is one of the most exciting events of their life," Dmitry had told me.

We shared that excitement, but we also found ourselves nearly overcome by claustrophobia. "What kind of parade is this?" Robert hollered to me as he attempted to maneuver his dog team through the crowd down the main street.

"Yeah," I laughed, "it's more like run for your life." I turned my double-layered caribou parka and beaded fur headdress into a suit of armor and thrust through the crowd to clear a parade route.

When we got to the town square, we were ushered onto a viewing platform. Even the dogs were hoisted up. They seemed to appreciate the escape from the hands of hundreds of admiring children. The relief was only temporary because soon the crowd followed us onto the stage.

At the back of the platform, the dogs had been secured to scaffolding that bore a large banner with the expedition logo. Wires feeding the loudspeakers were draped over the metal bars of the scaffolding. I looked back from our position on the platform in time to see our dog Kohojotak happily chewing through one of the electrical wires. I frantically rammed my way through the crowd and yanked the cord from his mouth just before he ended our sound system and possibly his life. We didn't know it at the time, but Kohojotak would have a more serious brush with death later in our journey.

As an announcer introduced us, the cheering grew louder. Hands reached up from every direction with gifts of pins and buttons and slips of paper for us to autograph. Then the platform started to shift under the pressure of the crowd. "I think we're standing on a fault zone," I said to Ginna. All I could think

25

of were those horrible tragedies at soccer matches in England and hundreds of people being trampled to death by surging crowds.

We began looking for an exit. I didn't want to become a casualty of *glasnost* and *perestroika*.

Fortunately, just before the situation reached crisis proportions, the native dance company of Anadyr began performing in another corner of the square. That relieved some of the pressure on the stage and gave us a chance to slip away into a side room of the auditorium.

There I asked Vadim how the dogs were doing. OK, he nodded, but then he said something in broken English that sounded like "eat two dogs."

"What?" I stammered back.

In the pantomime that followed, I gathered from Vadim that Cola's team had pounced on a couple of village dogs that had stumbled across our parade route. Vadim even convincingly played out a scene of a villager and the sled dogs playing tug-of-war with one of the unfortunate pets. I stared in disbelief. "Paul, no problem, very little dogs," Vadim said, holding his hands a foot apart.

I was never able to determine whether the village dogs had been eaten or just bitten, but the incident left me wondering what other problems we might encounter with our dogs.

In the theater that evening our team presented a program, the first of many we would give throughout our trek. The format was simple. We each told a little about ourselves and how we became involved with the expedition, and then we opened the program up for questions.

Saturday night's program revealed Dmitry's strengths as an outstanding public speaker. Beaming warmly at the audience, he punctuated his comments with deft gestures and well-placed pauses. Occasionally he engaged in banter with the crowd, drawing their affirmation of his comments. His presentation was compelling and persuasive. I had long wondered how he had managed so quickly to secure Soviet government approval for our daring, novel project, and now I had a clue.

On Sunday, while the rest of us continued preparing our food and equipment, Ginna, our team member from Anchorage, made significant headway on the diplomatic front. In a meeting with Nicolai Kashtikin, the top Communist Party official in Chukotka, she drafted a protocol calling for developments in trade, travel and communication between Alaska and Chukotka. Ginna's draft was a recommendation of objectives to be pursued by the governments of both countries. The objectives would lend substance to our efforts and serve as a focal point for our journey. Ginna did a superb job in preparing the protocol.

I had met Ginna in August, during my meetings in Alaska. She was one of the most knowledgeable people in the state about Alaska-Siberia relations. In early December, when I reported to her about my visit with Dmitry, I asked her for recommendations for a woman team member. She offered several names. A short time later she called back. She would like to be considered, she said. I learned that she not only had remarkable professional credentials but that she was also a superb athlete, an accomplished skier and an experienced camper. I offered her the spot, and she took leave from her job without pay.

While Ginna worked on the protocol, Dmitry coordinated logistical details. Caches of food and fuel had to be prepared for shipment to resupply points along our route. These would be sent ahead by helicopter. Reserve equipment had to be put in storage or sent ahead. Our radio communications network had to be fine-tuned.

Because rubles and dollars are not readily exchangeable, costs for this journey were being handled on what is known in Russia as a *bezvaluta* basis. Dmitry would be entirely responsible for all expenses and logistics on the Soviet side. I—with much help from Ginna—would cover arrangements for Alaska. To use the parlance common among current Soviet-American joint ventures, the business end would be handled through a "non-currency reciprocal exchange."

By Monday afternoon everything was almost ready. Dmitry still had work to do and needed Sasha's and Alexander's help.

I knew that Dmitry had more responsibilities in Chukotka than I had, but I was getting antsy. To have any chance of crossing the Strait by dog sled, we would have to arrive there by early April, when the ice and weather are most stable. Delays in our flight from Alaska already had put us a few days behind schedule, and we had at least a month's travel across Chukotka ahead of us. The tighter our schedule got, the less time we'd have for visiting the villages.

Dmitry agreed to my plan that while he, Alexander and Sasha stayed overnight to finish their work, the rest of us would head out to the edge of town and set up camp. That would give us a chance to become accustomed to the Soviet tent and cooking system. One of Dmitry's support staff who would be filming segments of our trek agreed to come along with us to help.

Anadyr officials offered to help move all of our equipment, sleds and dogs to the end of the road past the airport. They showed up at the sports hall with an amazing convoy.

The vehicles included a school bus, a panel truck, a platform truck, three jeeps and two tracked vehicles called *vizdahotes* that look like tanks without cannon. The locals were taking this operation very seriously. I was glad they did. The wind was coming up, and the road proved to be a roller coaster of deep ruts and chest-high snowdrifts.

By the time we reached the point where the road blended with the tundra, a blizzard raged about us. "Do you think we can set your tents in this storm?" I asked one of the members of Dmitry's support staff.

"No problem!" he replied with a carefree wave of his hand. "Now we have winds of maybe 25 meters per second. On Wrangell Island in the Arctic Ocean, Dmitry once put up that tent in winds of twice that speed. No problem!"

He was right. Within an hour after we were dropped off, camp was set with tents in place. All of us were comfortably nestled inside waiting for three Soviet gas stoves to make water from snow blocks for our tea and evening stew made of dried meat and *kasha*, buckwheat.

Cola was making last-minute adjustments to his sealskin dog harnesses. Zoya wielded needle and thread on a mitten. Others made diary entries while perched on coiled foam sleeping pads around the perimeter of the tent.

The American contribution to the homey atmosphere was a Coleman mantle lantern that cast its light from the ceiling.

Our Soviet friends marveled. They were accustomed to lighting their tents by candle.

I marveled at the ingenious simplicity of their tents. A dozen skis, placed upright in the snow, outline a 12-foot circle for the frame. A collapsible, umbrella-shaped top made of aluminum tubing slips over the ski tips, locking them in position. Then two shells—a breathable frost liner and an outer nylon fly—are draped over the frame. Snow blocks are piled on skirting around the base, and that anchors the structure in place. Plastic sheeting serves as the floor and is replaced every few weeks when it becomes soiled with food and fuel spills. The whole unit, minus skis, weighs less than 10 pounds. It pops up in minutes and provides ample room for more than a dozen folks to sit, or as many as eight to sleep.

Tonight, with three of our team members still in Anadyr, we needed only one tent. Generally we would put up two. One would serve as cook tent and quarters for those on kitchen duty, which would be shared by different Soviet-American pairs on a rotating basis.

After dinner and our two chocolates, packaged in blue wrappers featuring a smiling polar bear, Lonnie and I retired to our dog sleds. Nestling down in the sleds was something I'd grown fond of during the North Pole expedition. The sled offered comfort and privacy and relief from the snorers.

The three American sleds we had would all be used as sleeping quarters throughout the Bering Bridge journey. Robert would join Lonnie and me as one of the "regulars" who slept outside, but nearly everyone would give the sleds a try during the trip.

Our sleds were ideal as sleeping berths. Their tobaggon-shaped plastic bottom was just as long as a bed. The gentle upsweep in front formed a nice base for a pillow. When emptied of equipment each night, the full-length nylon cargo bag that stretched from the top of the handlebars in back to the brush bar in front provided shelter from the wind and snow.

Made almost entirely of aluminum and plastic, they weighed less than 50 pounds and could carry well over 500 pounds of payload.

The fourth sled, Cola's, consisted of a wooden platform on

aluminum stanchions and runners with no uprights or cargo bag. Loads were lashed on board, and it was steered by shifting the front end from side to side.

On Tuesday morning, March 7, with our first night's sleep in the outdoors behind us, we were finally ready to roll. The winds had abated. It was a 20-degree, overcast day.

As we dismantled camp and loaded our sleds, a press entourage arrived to see us off. For nearly an hour, jeeps, trucks and vizdahotes pulled up in steady succession. Like infantry dispatched to the front lines, photographers and videographers spilled out of the vehicles and rushed toward us with shutters clicking and cameras rolling. The crowd numbered nearly a hundred. Many of the journalists were from Moscow and had been waiting more than a week for this event. I would continue to be amazed throughout our journey at the interest shown in us by Soviet media.

The well-wishing, autograph signing and posing for photographs continued for nearly an hour.

I sought out Nicolai Kashtikin, the Chukotkan official who had been so supportive of our project. I had come to respect him a great deal. By all accounts, he was a truly progressive leader with a disdain for bureaucracy and a passionate regard for the welfare of people in his region.

As I went to shake his hand, he pulled me aside and said through an interpreter, "Remember, Paul, your journey is very important to us. It brings much hope to our region. All of us will be traveling with you in our thoughts."

Those words buoyed my spirits throughout our journey.

With a final wave, we pulled up the stakes that anchored our eager dog teams and headed out across the tundra.

We were finally under way, carrying our bridge-building efforts to the villages where the cultural connections between the countries mattered most. Our team was glowing with smiles. The first village, Uelkal, was 120 miles away. A northeast bearing along the inland side of mountains that line the Bering Sea coast would take us there. We expected it would take six days to reach our first town.

Cola's dogs performed beautifully on the trail.

The Soviet tent system was simple and ingenious.

Chukotkans track across the tundra in the vizdahote.

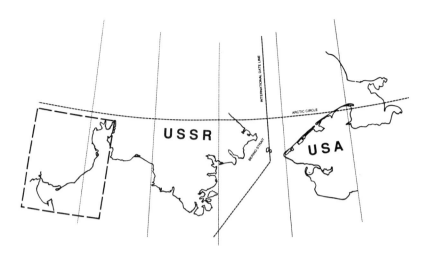

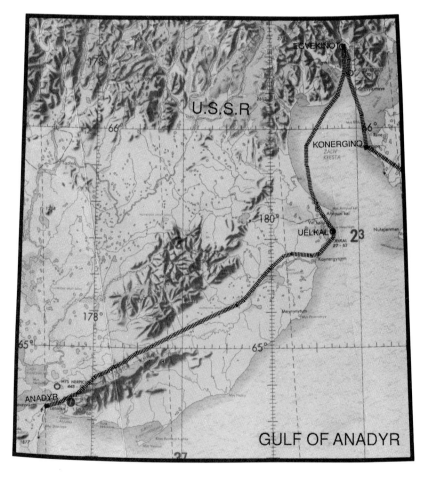

THREE

ТРИ

How great finally to be steaming across the tundra together! And what a multicultural caravan!

The four sleds were driven by Lonnie, Robert, Cola and Zoya. Interspersed among them were the eight skiers. Everyone carried a backpack with personal clothing and other items we might need during the day.

The dogs were as excited as we were to be on the move. The drivers had to ride their brakes to keep the sleds from overtaking the skiers.

Except for the short parade in Anadyr, this was the first time I'd seen Cola's dogs in action. There wasn't a purebred in the bunch—just a mix of big dogs and small dogs, dogs with long shaggy gray hair like miniature musk oxen and dogs with short tawny hair like German shepherds.

The dogs were powerhouses, though, and they were superbly trained. They responded instantly to all of Cola's commands—a mix of words, whistles and rasping sounds. He ran them side by side in four-dog and seven-dog teams. The only one I ever heard Cola call by name had the unlikely moniker of John Kennedy.

They were a contentious lot. Cola's dogs flashed their teeth and snapped any time our dogs were nearby. We'd better keep them separated, I thought.

The eight dogs we had brought from the U.S. were not as

well-trained as Cola's, but Lonnie and Robert seemed to have them under control. We had just got them eight months earlier. Lonnie had purchased them sight-unseen from the Canadian Eskimo settlement of Igloolik, an island just north of Hudson Bay. I had agreed to split the cost with him and become co-owner.

The dogs arrived in Minnesota with a set of labeled Polaroid pictures so we could match their Eskimo names to their faces. Because some looked much alike, it took us awhile to do that. It took even longer to figure out how to pronounce their names. Kirnik, Ojigilak and Taklak were black with white markings. Nattaqut, Siqo, Kitterut and Pikagulik were brown with white markings. Kohojotak, who together with Taklak was identified on the pictures as a lead dog, was distinctive. He was white with black speckles. Though initially skittish, they all proved to be friendly as they became accustomed to new surroundings. They had grown up in the arctic and had never seen trees before but soon learned how dogs put them to use.

All of our eight are purebred Canadian Eskimo freight dogs of peak pulling age, from two to six years, and average 80 pounds. Like all of their breed, they have long bushy coats and tails, broad chests, and faces with white "accent marks" just above their eyes. They make a strikingly handsome set.

They rarely bark. Rather, they howl, starting and stopping a long piercing chorus whenever they feel so inclined.

When we purchased the dogs, Lonnie was laying plans to launch his own expedition, a solo trek from the North Pole to Greenland. When the Bering Bridge plans got moved ahead a year, I asked him to become our sixth American team member. He agreed to postpone his plans for a year or two. A carpenter by trade, he is also an accomplished woodsman and a seasoned winter camper. His affable personality was proving to be a real asset among our eclectic crew.

A few hours into our journey, just when I had begun savoring the fact that we were finally on our own as a team, I noticed two figures far off to the right. The were wearing packs and were skiing parallel to our route. How did our team get separated so quickly? I wondered. And then, after looking back and counting noses, I realized that all 12 of our team members were ac-counted for.

"Hey, who are those two?" I yelled to Sasha. He squinted to look at them, thought for a moment, and then, with his char-acteristic sly smile, said, "KGB." Given his wry sense of humor, I could never be sure whether Sasha was being serious.

When I raised the question with Dmitry and Alexander, they appeared to be puzzled. As I continued to ski along, I pondered the identity of our two followers.

"Do you suppose they *could be* KGB?" I asked Ginna.

"It's possible," she said.

The prospect of KGB agents tracking us on this journey was disappointing. It suggested that Soviet government cooperation wasn't as genuine as it appeared.

The identity and mission of these two men, who would surface regularly on the trail and in towns across Chukotka, remained a topic of speculation throughout the weeks to come.

Early that afternoon our route took us past a small army outpost. Soldiers in long gray coats interrupted their target prac-tice to wave at us behind the fencing that enclosed a few ram-shackle wooden buildings and a couple of old tanks aimed at an artillery range.

"Greetings from America!" I shouted to them in Russian.

They waved back and smiled faintly. I wanted desperately to speak with them, but I sensed from Dmitry's demeanor that we'd best ski on by. Perhaps he felt we had strayed "out of bounds." He didn't say.

All of us were amazed that no one had stopped us from skiing so close to a military installation. It was true though, as Lonnie pointed out to me, that the outpost "sure doesn't look like a threat to our national security."

A short distance beyond we stopped for lunch. Our meal was accompanied by the rat-tat-tat of machine-gun fire as the soldiers returned to their marksmanship training.

The weather thickened as we pushed on. Out front of our group, I veered a little east from our compass bearing. I hoped to find a sheltered campsite in a river valley that led into the mountain range that lay between us and the Bering Sea. A few stunted bushes were the only windbreak we could find. We set camp among them.

That night, tucked in my sled bag and listening on a Sony Walkman to pop tunes by the California Raisins, I noted the stark setting in my diary:

"Here we are camped in the White Valley along the White River at the base of the White Mountains. This place is whiter by far than the Arctic Ocean, where at least there are blocks of blue ice to look at. It's far windier, too, with very changeable weather."

I also noted how positive my first impressions were of our team. Pulling 12 people together from across the globe so hastily was risky business. I wasn't sure it would work. So far it had.

The three Slavic Soviets all had polar expedition experience, and the native Soviets were obviously accustomed to life on the tundra.

The American team was less experienced. Only I had been on major expeditions, but everyone shared a commitment to the spirit of the Bering Bridge Expedition, and we were physically fit. Those were the prime qualifications. This wasn't a bunch of hard-core adventurers, but they didn't need to be. We weren't going to the North Pole.

Though circumstances would later prove me wrong, I didn't expect this to be a terribly rigorous journey. I knew, however, that it would be a complicated one, fraught with the difficulties of dealing with various cultures and government agencies as well as ever-changing trail and weather conditions. We needed a variety of skills, and what this American team lacked in depth we certainly made up for in versatility.

Ginna's diplomatic skills already had been indispensable. Lonnie and Robert were proving to be excellent dog handlers. Darlene's language skills would be essential when we reached the Eskimo settlements. Even on the first day it was clear that Ernie was one of our best skiers.

I thought back to how our three Alaskan Eskimos had become part of the team.

I met Ernie the previous spring at the Center for Northern Studies in Vermont. He was studying the anthropology of the

GINNA
Athlete and diplomat

Bering Region and the language roots of his Inupiaq people. In Ernie's hometown, Kotzebue, the largest Eskimo settlement in the U.S., he works as a commercial salmon fisherman in summer and substitute high school teacher in winter. Once he'd served as the mayor. Of slight build with small intense dark eyes and a reserved personality, he demonstrated an innate wisdom about the arctic and traveling through it that I knew would be an asset for our journey.

I met Robert in August when I traveled by helicopter from the Alaskan mainland to visit his village of Little Diomede. The village elders had recommended him to me as the best candidate. Though the modern accouterments of computers, cordless phones and video games now have their place among polar bear hides, harpoons and ivory carvings, everything in that village was still done under the watchful eye of the oldest men.

Robert was interested immediately. He was young and had little skiing experience, but was an excellent athlete, and I figured he could handle the rigors of the journey. Furthermore his cheery, easygoing demeanor and ready smile would serve all of us when times got tough on the trail.

Because he was a member of the Alaskan National Guard's First Scout Battalion, which watches Soviet activities on Big Diomede from surveillance posts on Little Diomede, Robert was well-versed in the U.S.-Soviet border issues. He also had a profound interest in making contact with native people across the Strait. Relatives of his, including an uncle who had taken up residence in Chukotka long before the border was closed, were thought to be still alive.

Both Ernie and Robert speak only a little of their native language, Inupiaq. Though the schools in their villages make an effort to teach it, it is no longer commonly heard in the homes. Thus Inupiaq young people have little incentive or opportunity to learn their language.

Among Alaskans of Siberian Yupik descent, native language skills remain strong. This is particularly true among the residents of St. Lawrence Island. Its two villages, Gambell and Savoonga, lie less than 40 miles from the Soviet mainland, and many of its older residents are direct descendants of Chukotkans.

Because Yupik represents the strongest cultural link between Siberians and Alaskans, it was imperative that our expedition include a Yupik Eskimo.

During my visit to Gambell in August, the Apangalook family was recommended to me as a source for our third native Alaskan team member. At first their son Ron, who had plans soon to get married, signed on. A few weeks before our departure, Darlene, his older sister, took his place. A student at the University of Alaska, she knew a little Russian in addition to Yupik. Darlene's family has many relatives among residents of the two key Yupik settlements in Chukotka—Sireniki and New Chaplino. Though Darlene was not a strong skier, her language skills and strong family connections with Chukotka would be invaluable.

We awoke the next morning, our first full day on the trail, to a cheery scene. The weather was calm and clear with temperatures in the teens. The ice-glazed hills and mountain peaks shimmered in the iridescent pastels of sunrise. We sat in a circle and enjoyed a picnic breakfast outside our tent.

It was March 8. Dmitry and I led out together.

Our progress was hampered by a series of steep ice grades. At midday that progress ended entirely. We found ourselves at the edge of an abyss, where the ridge line we were following was deeply gouged by a valley. Peering down the hundred-foot drop, Dmitry and I pondered our options.

"Let's go left. Let's get away from these foothills," I said, nodding toward the broad outwash plains.

Dmitry pointed out that our course was to hook slightly southward between the hills some distance ahead. He argued for hugging the base of the mountains and following a narrow, high rolling valley to our right.

The issue focused on just how close we were to a key pass ahead of us. Soon Sasha and Alexander joined our discussion. After examining our maps, we offered four astonishingly different opinions about our position.

Granted, the maps were difficult to read. For some reason, on these Soviet topographic maps, vague squiggles denote changes in elevation. I'm accustomed to the clean concentric rings found on American maps. Differences in maps, though, couldn't account for our vastly differing estimates of progress since leaving Anadyr. These estimates ranged from 10 to 25 miles. We looked at each other in dismay, all thinking the same thing: If we can't agree on something as basic as our rate of travel, how are we ever going to make a thousand miles together?

"All right," I said, "regardless of where we are, we know that it will be easier to travel on the flats than in the mountain foothills. Let's go to the left toward the valley. From out there in the open maybe we can spot a prominent mountain peak and determine our position."

"Yes, Paul, whatever you say," Dmitry responded grudgingly.

I set out northward along the rim. After skiing a short distance, I looked back to find that Dmitry had headed south with some team members and was out of sight over a hill.

The remaining team members were sitting by a sled, mired in confusion.

"What's going on here?" Ernie called to me.

"I'm not sure," I answered "but I think our co-leadership just hit its first snag."

Nearly an hour passed before we regrouped with Dmitry in a hollow at the base of the mountains. My anger showed as I looked ahead toward the series of rolling hills we would now have to traverse. Dmitry justified his actions by saying that while we had been looking at the map and discussing our choices, Cola had headed southward with his dog team and he had been obliged to follow.

I wanted to believe him, but I suspected the confusion had more to do with a battle of wills taking shape. Dmitry had questioned the notion of co-leadership with me many times.

41

That was understandable. He had never tried it before. As I had told him, though, this journey would hardly be an example of Soviet-American cooperation without equal representation of each country in the expedition's leadership. Clearly, it was going to take a lot of patience for us to sort out our partnership.

We continued on Dmitry's route for several miles, plodding uphill and down along the mountains until we came across a series of massive excavations. Perched on an undisturbed island of earth in the center of the diggings were a few homes.

"A gold mine," Sasha said to me, noting a symbol marked on his map.

Families emerged from the tiny dwellings. I could make out the figures of children waving to us as we detoured around the huge pits. A few fuel tanks and the rusting hulks of earth-moving equipment were strewn about.

"This is quintessential Siberia," I said to Lonnie.

"Yeah," he replied, "I wonder if those families have chosen to live there."

Chances are they had. Although we would later see remnants of forced-labor camps from the 1930s, we were told time and again that none still operated in Chukotka. We found most people willing to openly discuss that blight on the region's history, when so many lives had been destroyed in the camps.

More hills lay ahead. A swirling mix of fog and powdery snow reduced our visibility. Dusk was setting in.

From my vantage point on a hilltop it appeared that the next valley would offer us a sheltered campsite. As I skied on I realized there was no easy way to reach the next valley. We were at the edge of another steep drop.

Cola and I surveyed the embankment. We were looking for a negotiable route. The ground pitched a couple of hundred yards, and in some places the drop was nearly vertical. A ravine to the left looked like the least threatening option to me. By tacking back and forth, we might safely work our way to the bottom. I motioned to Cola that we try that route, but he had other ideas.

Cola maneuvered his sled to the top of a chute that dropped menacingly out of view into white nothingness. As I looked on, dumbfounded, Cola and Vadim hopped on the sled, straddling the load. Vadim nudged the sled over the edge.

"My God, what are you doing?" I yelled to them.

Much to my amazement, they were in control. Before they picked up much momentum, Cola jammed a stubby wooden pole between the planks at the front of his sled and into the snow. When he applied this brake, his momentum sent the back of the sled slewing around to the side, increasing his braking force. I watched, thoroughly impressed, as their sled moved safely down the valley wall, plowing up a billowy cloud of snow that hid them from our view.

Encouraged by their success, I helped Lonnie and Ginna move our sleds to the top of a less steep ravine to the left. We couldn't duplicate Cola's technique because our brake, which consisted of two sharpened steel pins mounted on a hinged flange, was on the rear of our sled. Our plan was to zigzag down the wall, but the first "zig" proved this plan unmanageable.

The sled raced out of control. We had all we could do to veer it uphill and bring it to a safe stop. Lonnie braced himself against the side of the sled to keep it from rolling downhill while I calmed the team. The dogs, who normally have no fear of scrambling up or down any grade, sensed our nervousness and were noticeably agitated.

"I tell you, Lonnie," I said, panting as I scrambled for ideas, "this suddenly feels like foolhardiness."

Way down below we could see a few tiny dark specks in the dim light. Team members on skis had managed to scramble to the bottom and were watching us.

I decided to try a technique that we'd used on our North Pole expedition to ease heavy cargo sleds down steep ramps of sea ice. I dug into the sled bag for the steel stake-out cables to which we clipped our dogs at night. We tipped the sled on its side and wrapped the cables around the runners as a makeshift brake.

Lonnie nosed the sled downhill as I led the dogs into position. Then, clinging to the back of the sled with our heels planted firmly in the snow, we began our descent again. The plan worked. Though the grade gradually steepened, we were able to hold a manageable pace. I had never taken a dog team down a grade as steep as this, but it worked, and we were exhilarated.

"Yahoo!" shouted Lonnie. From below we could hear other team members cheering us on. A sharp hump near the base of the hill sent us airborne, but the grade leveled out soon enough for us to regain control before the sled overtook the dogs.

I let out a triumphant howl and gave Lonnie a good rap on the back. Then we pulled into the spot where the others had already begun making camp.

"Good job. We enjoyed the show. So did our friends," said Alexander, pointing to our two mysterious companions looking down at us from a ledge halfway up the cliff.

In the morning over breakfast I opened a discussion about yesterday's progress. We had made only 15 miles.

"How can we push ahead more efficiently?" I asked.

It was clear to everyone that there was plenty of room for improvement. I know Dmitry agreed with that, but the suggestion of a meeting put him on the defensive. It seemed he felt his route decisions were about to be put on trial.

"Yes, Paul," he said, cutting me off abruptly, "I made a little mistake yesterday. We should have turned left away from the mountains, but you also made a little mistake. Many times there was great distance between our team members, and you did not stop and wait. I think this is not good."

He was right. It was important that we stay closer together. But it seemed that he would handle anything that smacked of criticism on this trip tit for tat.

We outlined a plan that would even out the pace: Lonnie and Robert would lead out with two American dog teams. Skiers would follow. Cola and Zoya would bring up the rear with the two Soviet dog teams. This order also would help prevent any spats between the Soviet and American dog teams. A few nasty incidents the day before made it clear to me that, even though we had been together for a few days now, the Soviet dogs remained intolerant of ours.

As we finished loading our sleds, I noticed our "KGB friends" had begun dismantling their camp on the ledge above us. "Good morning!" I hollered to them. "Please pack up quickly. We are ready to go." I figured that as long as we would be traveling together, we might as well try to be on friendly terms. They looked out from their shelter, waved to us and snapped a few pictures as we set out. We wouldn't see them again for several days.

The skiing and scenery were glorious that morning. A light dusting of snow had fallen overnight. The sunlight cut through bands of clouds and stippled the mountains and tundra with rosy patches.

I glided effortlessly along, enchanted by the ever-changing hues in this theater of light. It looked like we might be able to hit our stride and make our first 25-mile day. That was the pace we were shooting for. We had a tight two-month schedule to meet.

But the changeable weather took a nasty turn after lunch, and we found ourselves suddenly battling a stiff head wind that rapidly built into a blizzard. We put on our face masks and tightened our hoods to reduce the sandblasting effect of coarse, wind-driven snow. Blasts hit with such intensity that they drove us backward between each thrust of our ski poles.

Slinging our skis over our shoulders, many of us plodded along on foot. The visibility was less than 50 feet. I pulled out my compass and resorted to navigation by line of sight. Sasha and Ginna walked ahead of me, and every few moments I would yell out a course correction to them based on my compass readings. We made little headway.

Finally we gave up, deciding to set camp and sit out the storm. Quarrying snow blocks with a handsaw, we engineered a series of protective walls around our tents. In two hours our shelters were complete.

While the blizzard roared outside, we passed the afternoon in the tent. I pulled out my *Russian in Ten Minutes a Day* book. Zoya, sitting alongside me, offered to help. First we worked on the days of the week. Then came the chapter on the words for relatives.

When we started working on monetary units, Cola joined us. I learned about rubles and kopeks while he and Zoya learned about dollars and cents. Armed with a few new English words,

Cola let loose with the burning questions on his mind. "How much dollar one American car?" "How much dollar one house?" On and on his queries came as he pieced together a perspective on America.

Such language exercises helped us get to know each other. Our clumsy pronunciations of each other's words led to much shared laughter.

Music also helped. Included in our cargo was a guitar. We'd brought it from Alaska at Dmitry's request. "We always bring a guitar on our expeditions," he'd told me during one of our planning sessions in Moscow.

Lonnie and I spread our music books across the floor and sang a selection from the *Complete Book of Christmas Songs*, but our rendition of "Away in the Manger" brought only blank stares from our Soviet friends. Then we pulled out a Beatles song book and sang a rousing chorus of "I Wanna Hold Your Hand." Now *here* was a common language. The Soviets knew nearly every song in the book and sang them with us.

Then I passed the guitar to Vadim. What a delight to learn that he was a master of the instrument. He entertained us with a series of moving Russian ballads and flamenco style playing.

The next morning found us still stormbound. During the night, the winds had shifted to the south and that had brought sleet from the open waters of the Bering Sea, 10 miles away. The relentless wind had weakened the seams of our tent. Water dripped steadily from the ceiling, soaking much of our clothing and equipment. Our moods were decidedly less cheery as we tried to stay in the few dry spots and attempted to pass the morning with sleep.

"Still having fun?" I asked Cola as he wrung water from his socks. They had spent the night in a puddle in the tent corner.

"*Chute, chute*," he answered with a faint smile, using the Russian word that means "a tiny bit." We tried to make light of the situation but we all knew it could become serious. Being cold is something we could deal with, but being cold and *wet* is a far more serious situation. It can cause the body's core temperature to drop dangerously. The condition is known as hypothermia. We had the same concerns for our dogs. Several of us had gone out and cut snow blocks to protect them from the onslaught.

Late in the day our luck changed. The cloud cover thinned, and dry winds swept the camp. That evening the clouds pulled away from the western sky, allowing the sun to bathe us in crimson. We hurriedly fashioned tripods from skis and poles to serve as drying racks. Within minutes our sleeping bags, wind garments, mittens and hats were all dry.

Our Soviet team members were impressed. Initially they had been skeptical of the synthetic materials, including Thermax, Polar Plus and Supplex, from which my wife, Susan, had crafted our clothing system. Fabrics such as these are not readily available in the Soviet Union, and Dmitry, Alexander and Sasha weren't familiar with them and their benefits. They were more accustomed to expedition garments made from cotton, wool and down. The Soviet natives were more accustomed to furs.

But as we demonstrated outside our tent, the synthetic garments not only are far lighter and less bulky than ones made from natural fibers, making them easier to ski and work in, but also are less absorbent and dry amazingly quickly. Thanks to that quality we soon had dry clothes and sleeping bags—which let us get a warm and comfortable night's sleep.

The morning after the layover day we clipped along the trail, aided by a gentle downgrade and a steady tail wind. The dogs were outpacing the skiers, so I tied two ropes to each of the sleds.

"Now we'll have some fun," I said, offering ropes to the skiers. Though initially hesitant, they caught on to this technique—called *ski jouring*—right away.

Dmitry was particularly enchanted with it. "This is beautiful, very beautiful," he said as he glided along behind Zoya's sled.

Vadim and Sasha had the most fun, cutting gentle curves behind Cola's sled.

The strong wind swirled the snow in little rosettes across the ground and distorted my perception. At one point I thought I saw a large brown animal some distance ahead. A brown bear?

47

As I moved closer, I realized it was smaller and much too fast for a bear. It darted in zigzag fashion across the snow.

Perhaps a wolf? But then I realized it was smaller yet.

Ah, it must be a fox. Suddenly, just as I was about to step on it, I realized it was a lemming—a tundra animal not much bigger than a shrew. "So you're the little guy who's masquerading as a grizzly," I laughed.

I wasn't the first person to be tricked by the illusions of arctic light. Other adventurers have confessed to sightings of ships, buildings and even cities on the ethereal white landscape.

We saw no vegetation as we traveled. In the short weeks of summer, though—the snow-free season extends only from mid-June to early September—the poorly drained but nutrient-rich soil of upland tundra explodes with life and is carpeted in a thick mat of soggy lichen and wildflowers. Clumps of growth, called tussocks, form an ankle-bending obstacle course and make travel on foot here far more challenging in summer than it is in winter.

The vegetation provides browse year-round, not only for caribou and lemmings but also for a variety of other animals. These include arctic ground squirrels, whose soft skins are prized by the Eskimos for lining parkas; snowshoe hare and its larger cousin the tundra hare, which weighs up to 15 pounds; and game birds such as willow and rock ptarmigan and sharp-tailed grouse. Further up the tundra food chain, predators include wolverine, red fox and grizzly bear. Polar bears exist in the region but are likely to be seen only along the coastline, where their food staple, the seal, can be found.

We progressed more than 25 miles on that day. Our spirits were high. That night in the tent we predicted that we might top 30 miles the next day.

But come morning, Sunday, March 12, already our sixth day on the trail, the fickle weather once again chilled our optimism. Head winds, rain and sleet hampered us all day. As we slogged on, the soft sticky snow grabbed at our skis and sled runners. By evening we were exhausted and frustrated. We had never expected to encounter driving rains on the arctic tundra at this time of year. Our wind shells had been coated to make them water resistant, but they weren't waterproof. Gale force winds drove moisture into them that dampened our inner layers of clothing. Some team members battled chills. All of us grew edgy.

That evening I was mushing one of our teams when Cola brought his dogs alongside mine to pass. We'd learned already that letting the teams get too close together was a sure-fire way to start a dogfight. Just as the snarling and snapping began, I jumped between the teams and managed to separate the dogs. Livid with anger, I turned to Cola and screamed, "Don't you ever do that again! Do you understand me?" He glowered back at me and then pulled his team behind mine.

Though he couldn't understand English, he got the message. If a fight erupted, we risked severe injuries to our dogs. Cola had a tremendous amount of pride in his team. I think he felt that I was questioning his ability to control them.

After I cooled down, I regretted the incident. It set a rift between us that lingered for a long time.

On the other hand, the episode signaled that we had taken another step in the maturing process as a team. We could level with each other. The "honeymoon," during which we had carefully measured our words lest we risk offending one another, was over.

Generally, though, our relations were good.

Lonnie and Robert teamed with Cola and Vadim each night to parcel out rations of "pemmican" to our dogs. The dog food was a commercial mix of dried meat, fat and nutritional supplements that looked like liverwurst, packaged in two-pound cubes. The four handlers also chopped up slabs of frozen walrus and seal meat as an extra treat for our huskies.

Ginna and Sasha sorted through the team member's rations each day, meting out our breakfast oatmeal and our evening meal of dried meat and kasha. They also divvied up "finger food" for lunch. This included dried sausage, crackers, raisins, chocolate and honey.

The budding friendship between Ginna and Sasha had gotten its start in January, when Sasha had joined the American team members for a week's training at my home in Minnesota.

Zoya and Darlene took to each other right away and became

close companions. Though Zoya was old enough to be Darlene's mother, they were a great source of support for each other. Zoya often towed Darlene, who had difficulty maintaining our pace on skis, behind her sled.

The Yupik language link between them proved useful for the rest of us as well. In Anadyr, for example, I occasionally relied on them to help me speak to village officials when an interpreter wasn't present. Darlene would pass my message in Yupik to Zoya. She in turn would pass it to the official in Russian. It was a time consuming way to converse, but it did work.

It was also a lot of fun. As if playing a game of "telephone," we'd eagerly wait to see if the answers that returned to me via English, Yupik and Russian corresponded with the questions I had asked.

Among our team, we generally relied on Dmitry's, Sasha's and Alexander's knowledge of English for communication as a group. Delays for interpretation made for some convoluted conversations. Like so many other facets of the experiment in a cross-cultural project, discussions required a lot of patience.

I began the journey with a working vocabulary of about 50 Russian words. That quintupled during the next few months. That growth wasn't surprising. My choices were to smile a lot and feel stupid when Russian was being spoken—or make an effort to learn it.

The other two languages among our team members, Chukchi and Inupiaq, were rarely used.

To each other, Cola and Vadim sometimes spoke Chukchi, which has little in common with Eskimo languages. I wish I had learned more about Chukchi, which has some interesting features.

One difference involves the female and male pronunciation of some words. The word "no," for example, is pronounced *k'tsym* by men and *k'rym* by women. Another unusual feature is that the Chukchi counting system is based on the number 20, the number of a person's fingers and toes. Hence to count means literally to "finger." Twenty literally means "20 fingers" and 40 means "two sets of hands and feet."

Our camp routine settled into a rhythm. Dmitry's system

called for one American and one Soviet to tend to kitchen duty each day, making dinner in the evening and then getting up at 4:00 a.m. to prepare breakfast. The most time-consuming chore was melting snow in our cook pots to provide water for cooking as well as for our beverages—tea and coffee. According to the plan, each pair of people on cook duty took a turn every sixth day.

It worked well enough except that it didn't allow us to master the Soviet cookstoves. Operating them required a certain finesse. If the stoves weren't primed properly, raw gas and flames ran down onto the fuel tank and the wooden crate that served as our cooking platform. As long as the valve was shut down instantly, the fuel would burn itself out harmlessly in seconds. During the few times it had already happened, Dmitry had seemed unconcerned. But I couldn't help wondering how long the pressurized tanks of our three stoves could be enveloped in flame before they'd go off like a bomb.

The morning after I lost my temper with Cola my concerns about the stove were nearly realized. As I loaded a sled, I heard shouts of alarm in the tent behind me. Looking back, I saw the wall nearest me glowing from flames leaping inside. I raced toward the tent and yanked the fly out from under its anchor of snow. Reaching inside the tent, I pulled out the flaming stove and pitched it into the snow. The wooden box had caught fire and flames were spreading across the plastic tent floor. I grabbed the nearest source of liquid, our coffee pot, and doused the flames. After the smoke cleared, I noticed Dmitry was staring at me.

"Paul, why did you use our coffee?" he asked with a baleful look.

I stared back. I was speechless. We had perceived the hazard in profoundly different ways.

That surprised me because we saw eye to eye on many other leadership issues. Logistics, rations, configuration of sleds and skiers—on all these issues we had come to quick agreements. How could we view this stove incident so differently? I resolved that if we were going to be effective as co-leaders on this expedition, I simply had to get to know Dmitry better.

My effort started that morning. Skiing beside him, I opened

a conversation about our personal lives. I asked what he valued most in life.

"The love of family," he answered and talked glowingly about his two sons and how much they meant to him. In addition to Nikita, who had helped us in Anadyr and would meet us again later in the journey, Dmitry and his wife Tatyana also had a younger son, Matvay.

I told Dmitry of my admiration for his depth of experience. He is 14 years older than I and has led far more expeditions. There was much I stood to learn from him. We talked of arctic authors and of the explorers. We found that Roald Amundsen and Ernest Shackleton ranked as heroes for both of us.

The conversation was brief, but I treasured it because it was one of the few personal talks we had during the trek. Perhaps it was just because of the difficulty of communication, but he always seemed reluctant to discuss topics with me that weren't related to expedition logistics. I was able, however, to piece together more information about him and his life through press clippings and talks with his colleagues.

I learned that Dmitry was born in Moscow in 1941. He grew up in a section of the city that was frequently bombed during the war by German airplanes. His grandmother called him "little bomber boy" because she had often taken him to shelters during air raids.

His father, a professional writer, died many years before. His mother, a mathematician, still lives in Moscow and has been one of the most influential people in Dmitry's life. Following her footsteps, Dmitry studied mathematics at Moscow University and graduated with a gold medal. He began his career as a teacher in 1969 and holds a professorship in the mathematics department at the Moscow Institute of Steel and Alloys.

Dmitry's fascination with arctic trekking developed simultaneously with his career as a mathematician. He went on his first ski expedition when he was 28. He led expeditions in the Soviet arctic in 1969 and 1972. Then in 1979 he led a Soviet team on skis to the North Pole from Henrietta Island, one of the northernmost points of land in the U.S.S.R. For that accomplishment he was given his country's highest honors—the

Lenin Award and titles of Master of Sport and Lenin Komsomol Laureate.

Many other expeditions followed. In 1986 Dmitry and his team traversed a 400-mile stretch of the Arctic Ocean in mid-winter darkness. This "Polar Night" trek, which researched the secondary magnetic north pole, ranks in my opinion as one of the most arduous expeditions in recent decades.

Then in 1988 Dmitry led the "Polar Bridge" traverse of the Arctic Ocean from the Soviet Union to Canada.

Dmitry has authored four books about his journeys: *The Way North, Three Riddles of the Arctic, To the Pole* and *On Foot to the Top of the World.* None has been translated into English.

Dmitry's big dream—traversing Antarctica on skis— remains unaccomplished. He was nearly able to launch it in 1982. The plan had received the support of the Soviet government. A ship, helicopter and 200 tons of gasoline were sent to Antarctica in preparation. But in November, a week before Dmitry and his team were to depart, Soviet General Secretary Leonid Brezhnev died. The resulting turmoil in the Kremlin led to canceling the journey. Though Dmitry is beyond the usual peak expedition age, he remains determined to complete this project. Many times during our journey he spoke with me about this plan.

After days of soggy misery the trekkers dried their clothes in the wind.

Roomy tents were refuge from the storms and home on the trail.

Vadim delighted in his feast of the freshest of fish.

FOUR

ЧЕТЫРЕ

At the end of our seventh day, Monday, March 13, I searched the northeastern horizon in vain for a trace of Uelkal, our first village. Surely, I thought, we were within 20 miles, but out here among the rolling featureless hills of endless Siberian tundra, with no landmarks around us, it was impossible to know our position exactly.

We found the way the next morning. Just after breakfast, two ruddy-faced men wearing long canvas coats pulled up on a snow machine alongside our camp. How in the world did they find us? I asked. "We are hunters," one of them answered in Russian. "We know these hills like the back of our hands."

The mayor of Uelkal, they said, had asked them to look for us while they were out tracking caribou. They pointed out the correct bearing and said we had about 18 miles to go. That was exciting news. We knew we'd reach the village by early afternoon.

A few miles farther on, we found that the trail crossed a lagoon. Fishermen were seated behind snow shelters in the center of this expanse of ice. They greeted us warmly and invited us to try our luck for the small tomcod they were pulling up through the ice, which was two feet thick. The catch, they said, was for their dog teams.

Vadim was quick to show us that, when filleted, the raw flesh of these hand-sized fish makes a good trail treat for people as well. The best part, he said, are the eyes. He proceeded to nibble them out of several fish that were still flopping. "Very good, maybe you like," he said, holding out a one-eyed fish for Ginna and me to try. She declined, but I took a taste. It had no flavor but the texture was . . . interesting. One try was enough.

The trail into Uelkal took us along the shore on a sand ridge, giving us our first close-up view of the Bering Sea. Its surface was a chaotic mass of fractured rubble ice, but it appeared to be firmly frozen. Blocks the size of steamer trunks lay strewn across the surface. The scene was invigorating. I flashed back to my polar journey and thought of how inviting this rubble would have looked to us compared to the massive 12-foot-high pressure ridges we had encountered on the 1986 trek.

Two miles from town we were met by a group of photographers, who introduced themselves as the "advance welcoming committee" and said they would be filming our arrival. They greeted us warmly and then escorted us by snow machine into town.

The dogs—their curiosity piqued by new smells—ran faster. Skiers raced to keep up or grabbed tow ropes to catch a ride. Suddenly, just behind me, a dog fight exploded.

Cola was trying to pass one of our teams again. As we pulled apart the writhing, snarling mass of fur and teeth, I lost my temper and screamed at him. "What gives? Are you determined to see our dogs destroy each other?"

Our escorts looked on, astonished. What a terribly embarrassing scene! We'd been so excited about reaching our first village. Now our grand entry had been marred by this ugly fight. The episode had been made uglier still by my outrage.

Back under way, I sorted through my exasperation by talking over the problem with Sasha. "Why does Cola insist on doing that? Why can he not understand the problem?" I asked.

"I don't know," Sasha answered. "Perhaps it is something psychological."

He pointed ahead at Cola, who was coaxing his dogs ever faster toward the settlement.

Then I realized what was going on. It was simply a matter of pride. It was vitally important to Cola that his dogs be in front, especially when we were about to enter a village in his region. I decided to invite Cola to lead us into villages from here on.

At the edge of town was a military listening post with a huge rotating radar screen. It looked like the Distant Early Warning Line stations that dot the north coasts of Canada and Alaska. Our escorts led us right alongside it. Amazingly they didn't caution me against taking photos. Nor did they stop Ginna, who was dutifully documenting the scene with our video camera. I did learn later, though, that one of the Soviet journalists said to her that this was "not the best place" to shoot film.

Nonetheless, even Dmitry was surprised at the nonchalance of our escorts. In a country that forbids its own citizens to take pictures of military installations, aircraft or even airports, we were amazed that we were allowed to take pictures of a defense installation on a strategic stretch of Soviet coastline. I suspect the rules were simply overlooked because of the joy the villagers felt about our visit.

As we drew closer, the military officers and their families came out to greet us. They gathered around our sleds to get their pictures taken with us and our dog teams.

The quarter-mile trail that led from the army camp to the settlement was lined with hundreds of cheering people. "This is it!" I hollered to the team. "This is the moment we've been waiting for. This is what this trip is all about." A warm glow washed over me as we moved on toward the cheering crowd.

Suddenly the sky flared with color. Someone had set off a volley of fireworks. The dogs panicked. Half of them hit the dirt, and the other half turned tail and ran back, wrapping all the teams in a snarl of lines. Sasha ran ahead to the village waving frantically to preempt any plans for more fireworks.

We gathered the dogs and proceeded to drag the shellshocked animals through the cheering mob. People pulling dogs—now that was a real crowd pleaser!

Uelkal consisted of a few brightly painted apartment blocks and several dozen little homes with steeply pitched wooden roofs and whitewashed plaster walls. Our expedition gathered in a little square in the middle. A young blond Slavic Russian introduced himself as the mayor and gave a welcoming speech through an interpreter. "The people of this village have long felt friendship toward America," he said.

He explained that the older villagers remembered well the Americans who had stopped here during World War II with the lend-lease materials that were being delivered to the Soviet Union's western front via Alaska. "We have felt a special connection to America ever since then, and your arrival has assured us that the feelings are the same across the sea," the mayor concluded.

Then the crowd cleared a space for the village's Eskimo dance troupe. Twelve younger women—the dancers—wore long bright blue coats accented with beadwork and fur. Six older women—the drummers—wore similar costumes in orange and yellow. Some of them had tattoos on their chins and cheeks. They half sang, half chanted songs while striking a tambourine-like drum made of walrus hide. The dances reminded me of those performed by South Sea Islanders. The dancers' hands cut descriptive pirouettes, gracefully weaving a story in the air, as the dancers gently bobbed in time with the music.

Robert, standing next to me, tugged my sleeve. "I know that dance. We do the same one back home—just the same," he said excitedly as his hands traced the movements of the dances.

The lead dancer addressed the crowd in the Eskimo language. Darlene nodded in recognition. "They are Yupik Eskimo, the same as my family," she said. "I didn't expect to find any here." She thought that only the settlements closer to Alaska included Yupik people.

From the mayor we learned that Uelkal is the westernmost Eskimo community in the world. Thinly spread from Uelkal to the east coast of Greenland are the villages in which the world's 50,000 Eskimos live.

However Uelkal is not a traditional village site. It was established relatively recently. A famine in the early 1930s sent Eskimos from the village of Chaplino looking for better hunting grounds. At this spot, nearly 200 miles west of their original home, near the mouth of a large bay, they found rich grazing lands with ample caribou and a sheltered lagoon that is frequented by walruses and whales. So here in our first village, where we didn't expect it, Robert and Darlene discovered traces of their cultural heritage.

The dancers presented a gift to each member of our team—slippers, booties, gloves and pendants—made of fur. They were decorated in beadwork. We shook hands or hugged nearly every member of the crowd and then were escorted to the town hall, a small white building that looked like a cottage. A huge Soviet flag was posted near the door.

The mayor, Vadim Manokov, led us into the council chambers, a meeting room crowded with a long hardwood table and numerous hand-painted wall posters with the insignia of the Communist Party.

"Will this do?" Dmitry asked me.

"Will this do for what?" I responded.

"The mayor would like us to stay in this room. He says it will be a great honor for the community if we do."

With a broad smile, the mayor confirmed what Dmitry was telling me.

"It is perfect," I said, thanking him profusely in Russian, though I shuddered at the thought of what this room would look and smell like after we spread out our soggy garb.

Then we were led to another building, a low squat house with high narrow windows and dark blue trim. Like so many buildings in the village, it had been shifted and buckled by frost heave. Inside, we were seated around a dining table in a dimly lit room. Three cooks, matronly women wearing long white coats and billowy white scarves, emerged from an adjacent room where the crackling of a wood cookstove could be heard.

Platters of whole fried finger-length fish that looked like smelt were set before us along with bowls of something like ravioli in a sauce. We were ravenous. The food was outstanding. We ate till we were dizzy.

Robert wolfed down the fish, fins and all, as fast as they were brought out. "I'm really feeling at home now," he muttered between bites. The cooks watched in delight as we devoured the food.

After our dinner in Uelkal we were treated to luxurious hot

baths in the homes of various townspeople. My bath was in a nicely appointed flat owned by the regional game warden and his wife, the village librarian. He proudly presented me with his personal hunting knife. I was honored but felt bad that all I had to offer in return was a rinky-dink pair of folding pliers.

From another guest, amateur photographer K. Lemeshev, I received a set of black and white photos depicting the region and the people who live there. "These are not fancy pictures," he said to me. "This is our life as we see it. Please share them with people in America."

I was deeply touched. This was one of those spontaneous moments that would make this expedition special.

Other team members enjoyed similar moments. An older woman told Alexander, "You have given me back my youth."

"How's that?" he asked.

"Because when I was young I saw the Americans come to us and now I again see them come to us. Thank you. You have given me back my youth." With that she broke into tears.

Ernie said that the tremendous relief that he felt getting off the trail and reaching this village was ironic to him. "From what I'd been taught in school about the Russians being our enemy, I never thought I'd feel so safe reaching one of their communities."

Later that evening our team gathered on the stage of the local community hall to talk with the packed throng about our project. The audience, an equal mix of natives and non-natives, was intensely interested. They hung on every word and asked many questions: How do you like our village? How does it compare with the villages in Alaska? Will other Americans visit us?

Afterward, our native team members stayed on to join the Eskimos of Uelkal for a celebration of native dancing and native foods. Darlene, much to her delight, found that she had a few distant relatives here.

In the morning I hiked out on the sea ice to set up our radio antenna. Nearly two weeks had passed since our arrival in Anadyr, and we had yet to make good radio contact with our base in Nome, Alaska. Every evening we had strung our antenna

ALEXANDER
A touching moment

on ski poles across the campsite and huddled around our single sideband radio hoping to hear the voice of Anne Walker, our publicist and base coordinator back in Nome. The radio and antenna should have been ideal for transmission over these distances, but only once had we made brief and garbled contact.

In addition to the perplexing technical radio problems, we also had some political ones. In Anadyr, Dmitry had informed me that we had yet to secure formal approval from the Soviet Ministry of Communications to transmit to the U.S. on our commercial-band radio. This was one of the many complications that resulted from moving the project a year ahead of schedule.

Amateur-band approval had been received, and Alexander was able to relay messages to ham operators in Alaska through the Soviet base station, but relays via four radios and two languages weren't keeping our American followers informed of our progress.

Dmitry, concerned about possible repercussions from our unauthorized transmissions, frowned on our attempts to reach Alaska with commercial-band radio. Thus we kept our efforts low key. Here in Uelkal I crouched behind a large block of ice beyond view of the army camp as I attempted—to no avail—to make contact.

Later, when I thought back on this scene, it seemed silly. But it reflected the lingering misgivings I had about the extent to which the Soviet government trusted our presence in Chukotka.

The next morning while loading the sleds, we enjoyed some final moments with the townspeople. Our schedule allowed us only a one-night visit to this and most of the other towns along our route.

School children, who had been given the morning off so they could help us load sleds, gave us a tiny stuffed toy dog. We tied it on the prow of our lead sled as a mascot. I pulled out a handful of friendship stickers featuring a crossed-flags emblem and the words *Peace on Earth* in English and Russian and handed them out to the crowd.

Darlene passed her set of earphones around, letting the villagers sample the sounds of Bruce Springsteen through her Sony Walkman.

Ginna fielded questions from a circle of women, who were especially interested in women's rights in America.

As we skied out of town I shouted in Russian to the crowd. "We look forward to seeing you soon in Alaska." We were on our way to Egvikinot, a town of several thousand people some 60 miles north at the head of the bay. On our first day out of Uelkal, we clipped along the shoreline. Many of us, even with our backpacks, could skate-ski on the crusted snow. Out in front, I belted out every folk song I knew at the top of my lungs.

The next day, more excellent trail conditions, this time across smooth ocean ice, brought us within 20 miles of Egvikinot.

Our entourage now included an additional musher and dog team. In Uelkal a 33-year-old Eskimo hunter named Slava Practina had approached Dmitry, saying that a project like ours was something he had dreamed about being part of all his life. He wanted to know if some of our team members could stop by his house so he could get a picture of them with his dog team. Dmitry offered him one better, inviting him to travel with us for a few days.

Now, smiling broadly and chatting merrily to his 10 dogs, Slava bounded along in front of us, breaking trail with an ancient sled of steel and wood. By carrying part of the load from our sleds, he helped to increase our pace.

As we skied on toward the town, a press corps arrived to greet us by helicopter. They circled overhead so closely that the prop wash knocked some of us down. Dmitry raised a fist in

SASHA
A few choice words

anger. Sasha taught me my first few words of Russian profanity. "Now you know what to say the next time that happens," he said with a laugh.

The derricks of shipping cranes and plumes of diesel smoke that we could see from five miles out told us that Egvikinot was not a pastoral Eskimo settlement like Uelkal. Nonetheless, the setting was spectacular.

Egvikinot is nestled in a cleft of the spectacular chain of rugged mountains that surround the head of the bay. As we approached the town, dozens of villagers—mostly children—met us on skis. I was amazed at their skill. Though we had seen no sign of skis in Uelkal, skiing was obviously a popular sport in this town.

The entourage mushroomed as we reached the wharf, where we were formally greeted with bread and salt. "We will help you build the bridge," announced a community leader. "We are now part of your team."

We spread out our gear in the gymnasium. The dogs were staked out in the hockey rink. There they received the affections of dozens of children. Fortunately the dogs behaved themselves and no one was hurt.

Following a banquet at the school, I set off on a mission. I was determined to reach the U.S. by telephone to seek help from the State Department on our radio licensing problem. I asked the local English teacher who was serving as our interpreter if it was possible to place such a call. He looked at me incredulously. "I don't know. No one has ever tried," he said. "But let us find out what opportunities glasnost has opened for us."

From the home of the newspaper editor, our interpreter

contacted the regional operator. The operator said she would try to put the call through and would call us back with the results. Twenty minutes later the phone rang. I picked it up. My Soviet hosts gathered close around me. "What do you hear?" they asked, excited that their home was now connected with the U.S.

I pressed my ear to the receiver. Over the static I listened to a faint recorded message from our base in Nome, Alaska. Though Nome was only about 400 air miles away the message had traveled nearly around the world—via Philadelphia and Moscow—to reach us.

"You're not going to believe this," I answered them, laughing. "But what I heard from America was a weather report for Egvikinot and an announcement of our arrival here." I explained to them that Anne Walker apparently had received that information from a Soviet radio relay and had put it on her answering machine as an update for the media.

That night I told the story to the audience at our community program. "The Bering Bridge must already be in place," I said as I explained that I had received information about their village when I called Alaska.

The standing-room-only crowd rushed the stage afterward and gave us many gifts. My favorite was a copy of a book. Its title, loosely translated, is *Learning Hockey Without Tears.*

A dinner followed in the town's restaurant. We were treated to a fabulous banquet that included roast reindeer and marinated salmon and for dessert a beautiful torte in the shape of a large turtle. "We do not mean this to suggest that you are slow," laughed our host, "but rather that your determination is as strong as a turtle's."

After dinner I slipped next door to see how the average "Egvikinotian" spends a night on the town. I felt as if I had stepped into a scene from the 1940s. About a dozen couples were seated at small candlelit tables, being served by waitresses in evening dresses. Off to the side was the dance floor, a dark cave-like alcove lined with black carpeting. A few colored lights flashed in the corners.

An older formally attired couple was dancing around the floor to a Russian rock tune with an East Indian beat. A drum set along one wall was evidence that on other nights a live band played here.

Later that night, we were claimed by various townspeople who took us to their homes for socializing. I found myself back at the newspaper editor's home with our interpreter and several other Soviet couples. Would I consider a proposal from them? they asked. They had recently established a touring club to promote rafting, camping and backpacking trips in Chukotka. Perhaps I could help them organize a program for American tourists. Their plans called for a two-week raft journey down a river through Chukotka's interior. They would cover all ground costs for a dozen Americans if I, in turn, would cover ground costs for a reciprocal fishing trip for Chukotkans in the U.S. "In Siberia we have more than 500,000 rivers," one of them said to me. "The salmon and trout fishing is very good. Do you think this would interest Americans?"

"It certainly will," I said, smiling and thinking about what a passion fishing is for people in the north woods where I live.

I was struck by the determination of the people in Eg-vekinot. Tourism is their most promising source for foreign currency. We agreed in principle to work together on a pilot reciprocal fishing trip.

Situated at the base of a rugged mountain, Egvikinot had the quaint charm of an alpine village. Public buildings, like the Culture Palace where our program was conducted, are richly decorated with terra cotta friezes on the stucco exterior. A few of the town's steeply sloping streets are organized as wide boulevards with playgrounds for children on the medians. A trail leads uphill behind town to a ski area complete with a pink chalet, tow ropes and Bavarian music.

Also on the mountain slope was a granite spire, a memorial to two American pilots of the lend-lease program who lost their lives when their plane crashed in these mountains in the early 1940s.

I asked my hosts about the handsome fieldstone buildings I'd seen among the tall concrete apartment and office buildings in the center of the community. Those were remnants of a prison that existed here before the port was opened in 1951, they explained. The buildings had been erected by forced labor. "But mind you," said one of my hosts, "mostly they were legitimate prisoners here—thieves and such."

Dmitry and I set aside the next morning for a major strategy session. It was Saturday, March 18. With our maps spread out across the floor of the gymnasium, we set a revised schedule for the expedition. Five hundred miles and a dozen villages still lay between us and the International Date Line. With nearly two weeks of trail experience behind us, we knew our team could average 25 miles each travel day. Adding on another week's time for bad weather and rest days in some of the villages meant we would reach the International Date Line near the middle of April. Government officials in both countries were eager to learn of our target date so they could plan a crossing ceremony.

Dmitry and I agreed on a plan, which called for reaching the city of Provideniya, a major stop, on April 1. Our arrival at the International Date Line would fall from April 12 to 14. Getting there that late would mean the ice conditions would be marginal at best. We'd also be pushing our luck with snow conditions in Alaska. But we had little choice. All we could do was hope for the best and make the most of our time. The completion of the journey in Kotzebue, Alaska, was projected for May 1.

Little discussion was needed regarding the itinerary. Our projections were remarkably similar. Though he and I hadn't been able to connect well on a personal level, I found it gratifying that we were able to come to terms easily on issues concerning planning and logistics. It was clear to me that the language of adventure transcends cultural obstacles.

We departed Egvikinot with a fourteenth companion. Now not only did we have Slava, our Eskimo musher from Uelkal, but Dmitry's son Nikita as well. Nikita would ski with us during his two-week spring break from his university studies in Moscow. I enjoyed his company. He had inherited his father's charm and drive and bubbled over with excitement about taking part in our project. "This is a dream for me," he said as we skied along together. "Like my father, I have always wanted to travel in the arctic but I never dreamed that my first journey would be with such a remarkable group." His English was quite good, so with his help my Russian took a quantum leap.

Our next settlement, Konergino, was only 35 miles away. We reached it the day after leaving Egvikinot. The location had been used for centuries as a place for rounding up reindeer, though this village, like the other two we had visited, was formally organized in the 1940s, when the semi-nomadic Chukchi people were encouraged to settle in communities. *Konergino* is a Chukchi word that means "reindeer corral."

Konergino is similar in size to Uelkal but has a strikingly different feel. As Robert said, "This place has odd vibes."

His suspicions began with the ceremonial fire that was part of the welcoming festivities. We were told that it was intended to ward off bad spirits that might have accompanied us into town.

A few of the native people who gathered around us in the town square were quite obviously inebriated, though in fairness I must say that this was the only example of public drunkenness that we saw in Chukotka.

We learned later that one reason for the malaise in this town was that two of their young people had drowned in the Bering Sea two weeks before when the supply truck they were driving across the ice from Egvikinot broke through and sank.

In the town's tiny restaurant we were formally greeted by the director of the town's collective farm, a portly man in black coat, hat and scarf who had the air of a Mafia chieftain. Locals later confirmed our feelings, telling us that he was the self-appointed czar of the region's caribou industry, a significant part of the economy in Chukotka.

"He took control but not by popular vote," one villager said to me with a hint of anger in his voice.

Our visit was marred by another unfortunate incident with one of Cola's dogs. I was organizing our equipment in the school gymnasium when townspeople carried in a small Chukchi boy and laid him on a mat. "Quick—we need help! This boy was badly bitten!" Lonnie yelled over to me.

We grabbed our first-aid kit and then, under Zoya's supervision, cleaned the boy's wounds and bandaged him up. He was sobbing uncontrollably. I slipped my Sony Walkman on him to help distract him while we worked.

The incident made me angry. The night before the same dog had snapped at Robert. When we finished bandaging the little boy, I discussed the situation with Dmitry. It was obvious that this dog couldn't be trusted around strangers. "Why don't you insist that Cola isolate this animal when we enter villages?" I asked.

Dmitry's response startled me. "It's not Cola's fault," he said. "The problem is with the children. They must learn not to come near the dogs."

"That attitude will never work in Alaska," I said, thinking about the liabilities we might face if an Alaskan villager were injured by our dogs.

"OK, we will leave all Soviet dogs in Chukotka and take only your dogs with us into Alaska," he snapped back, flashing an angry glare.

"That's not the point," I said. "The issue only concerns one dangerous dog. It's not a case of Americans versus Soviets."

Our discussion continued along these lines for some time but got nowhere. We found that whenever our discussions about problems took on nationalistic overtones our ability to talk about them rationally deteriorated rapidly.

Our visit to Konergino was not without its bright moments, though. One was the disco late that evening after our community program. The occasion included not only dancing but games as well. Lonnie took on the locals in a challenge of who could be the first to whistle after gobbling down a huge piece of cake. "Boy, that was tough! I was blowing crumbs all over the room." In another game, he had to stick a sliding box cover over his nose and pass it to his teammates' noses without using hands. "That one got us good and close," said Lonnie.

Dmitry—ever the diplomat—drafted a letter in Konergino outlining our project and progress. We co-signed the letter and sent it to the Kremlin and the White House. Addressed to both

General Secretary Gorbachev and President Bush, our letter from Konergino read as follows:

We are pleased to announce the launching of the Bering Bridge Expedition. This unprecedented example of Soviet-American cooperation began in Anadyr, the capital of Soviet Chukotka, on March 7.

Our team of six Soviets and six Americans will travel by ski and dog sled along a 1,200-mile route linking the native settlements of the Soviet Far East, traversing the sea ice of the Bering Strait and then continuing through the villages of western Alaska.

Three Bering Region natives from each country are included among our team to represent the strong cultural link between Asia and North America in this region. Every element of this project is focused on forging bonds of friendship, building a bridge based on common needs. Friendship has historic traditions in this region of peace and friendship that comes from the unity of culture and blood bonds.

We believe that the Bering Bridge will be rebuilt and that someday soon our mutual border will be guarded by friendship alone. We have high hopes that our efforts will hasten the improvement of Soviet-American relations for peace on our planet.

Tomcod fishermen invited the travelers to drop a line.

The mountainsides spilled into Egvekinot.

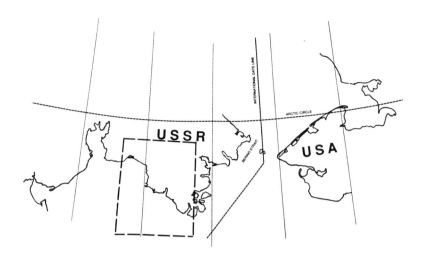

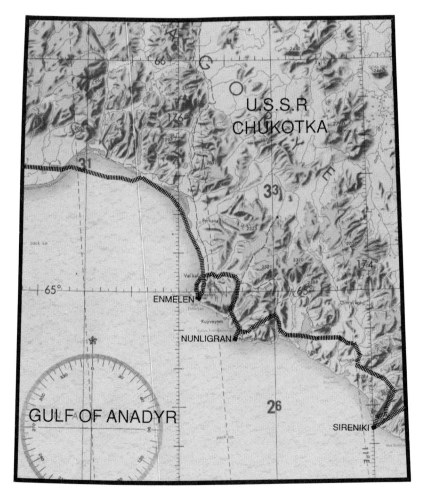

FIVE

ПЯТЬ

From Konergino we embarked on a seven-day trek over tundra and sea ice to reach Enmelen, 150 miles away. A Chukchi herder who accompanied us out of town by snow machine told us that along the way we would pass by the free-ranging caribou herds that his village managed. Buoyed by the anticipation of eyeing thousands of these animals—the heart, soul and sustenance of the Chukchi race—we set a brisk pace across the rolling tundra.

Just after noon, while Dmitry's son Nikita was skiing beside me, teaching me the words to the Soviet national anthem, I saw the distant horizon move. It looked like an ocean wave. Squinting, I realized this was a caribou herd. With camera slung over my shoulder I left the group and scurried off toward the mass of tawny animals. I wondered how close I dared approach. Would the sudden appearance of a bright blue figure on skis startle them into a stampede? And would I then become a bright blue imprint on the tundra?

As I approached, the caribou showed no alarm but continued pawing up the snow and foraging on the moss below. I was amazed at their variations in color. Some were a deep russet, some tan, some chalk white and others the mixed colors and patterns of an appaloosa.

An even more spectacular scene awaited us later that evening. Cresting a ridge, we saw before us a vast plain dotted with caribou. The mountains behind them were painted in mauve by the setting sun. A sliver of moon and wispy clouds arranged in graceful swirls accented this pastoral vista. I was awestruck.

Adding to the magic, a Chukchi herder was patrolling the perimeter of the herd by dog team. Lonnie and I beckoned him over to us. He approached, shook our hands and then looked on with pride as we admired his team and his dogs.

I recognized the beautiful and ancient design of his sled from drawings I'd seen in books of Chukchi culture. The runners were long driftwood poles sheathed with strap iron. A raised platform of wooden planks was lashed to arched stanchions cut from caribou antlers. Two bands of baleen—cut from the inside of a whale's mouth—curved up from the front of the runners and connected with the platform.

The herder's six small dogs sat attentively. Like the caribou, they were surprisingly varied—large and small, black and white, short-haired and long. But their performance was impressive. When the herder hopped on his sled and gave a quick guttural command, he and his team went racing across the tundra, bounding airborne over every ridge of snow.

We pitched our tent near the herder's camp. In honor of our visit, the two Chukchi men tending the camp invited Vadim and our trail companion to butcher an animal of their choosing for a feast. With knife in hand they set out walking among the herd and, an hour later, returned with selections of fresh meat for our stew pot.

The next day the calm clear weather gave way to another windstorm as we left the camp. By afternoon we found ourselves battling head winds that nearly swept our feet out from under us. I was out in front with Ginna, Sasha and Lonnie and, unfortunately, had allowed our group to spread out again. At three o'clock we stopped and waited 30 minutes before the next batch of skiers and sledders arrived. Dmitry was alarmed. For more than an hour he had seen no sign of Robert and Darlene. I jettisoned my backpack and backtracked to find them. The others agreed to continue forward for an hour and set camp.

As I skied back on the faint tracks that our sled runners had cut in the wind-packed snow, I remembered that the Chukchi had said that polar bears had been seen roaming the coast.

I wondered if Darlene and Robert had encountered one. The wind continued to build, all but obliterating the track I was following. Those faint marks were my only link to safety. I felt foolish to have allowed myself to get into such a hazardous situation.

Eventually I came upon Robert and Darlene, ambling along with one of our dog teams. They responded with complete nonchalance to my shout of relief. "Oh, we just got a late start after the lunch break," said Robert. It had never occurred to them that to be an hour behind the rest of the crew put us all in jeopardy. As Dmitry would often point out to me, such incidents were the price we paid for having included young and inexperienced adventurers on the American team.

When we reached camp, the team was laboring to build a series of massive snow walls to protect our tents from the fierce winds. Three times the walls had blown over. It was well after dark before we finally had camp secured.

Later that night the storm caused another brush with disaster. A slight shift in the wind exposed one corner of the cook tent to the wind. We used extra skis to brace the badly listing wall. As drifts piled up outside, pressure mounted on the nylon fabric. Suddenly a seam burst. Several team members dashed out and worked feverishly to reinforce our snow walls.

Over breakfast in the morning, as Zoya sewed the torn seam, Dmitry noted that the crew repairing the walls last night included only Soviet team members. "These tents may be Soviet equipment but for the next two months they are homes for all of us. Everyone must work together," he admonished us.

Throughout the morning the storm ebbed and surged as we pushed onward. In the valleys the wind was so intense that some of us had to lock arms with each other.

"Well we've finally found a way to keep this team together," I told the crew.

The dogs—their eyes smarting from a relentless blasting of snow and their trail-tracking instincts numbed by the blur—wandered aimlessly off course. From time to time we'd rotate different dog teams to front position.

Our hoods, face masks, scarves and goggles were carefully adjusted to protect our flesh from the stinging blast. Snow packed into our goggle vents and froze onto our sunglasses, requiring frequent scrapings.

By early afternoon, our progress had been reduced to less than a mile an hour. It seemed futile to push onward, but it seemed equally futile to try organizing a camp in these conditions. We had one other hope. The Chukchi herders had told us of a hut somewhere in this vicinity. Finding it seemed hopeless. Amazingly, in late afternoon we stumbled upon an orange shack half buried in snow.

As we approached two men poked their heads out the front door to greet us. Our "KGB friends." They had been waiting out the storm here since yesterday. I still was skeptical about their identity but for once I was delighted to see them. We followed them into the tiny quarters, where they offered us tea.

A massive wood stove and two narrow sets of bunk beds took up most of the space. Faded pictures of Soviet movie stars adorned the walls. While Cola and Darlene prepared fish stew from a couple of slabs of Dolly Varden trout from the dog food cache on Cola's sled, we chatted with our new friends. Though other expedition members had spoken with them before along the trail, this was the first time I'd had a chance to talk with them. They introduced themselves as Kosta and Vlodya.

"We're avid sportsmen," Kosta said, with Alexander as interpreter. "We wanted very much to be part of your expedition, but when we found out we couldn't, we decided to ski along your route." Sounds like a good cover, I thought to myself. I was still suspicious. So was Lonnie. He winked at me.

Kosta and Vlodya said they were from the village of Neshkan. That is where Cola and Vadim live. When I noted that, Kosta responded, "Yes, I am Cola's brother-in-law."

Cola nodded. I looked on incredulously. How was it that some of us didn't know that? Why hadn't they introduced themselves to us the first day? Why was it I hadn't noticed Vadim and Cola make much effort to visit with them before this? And why had Dmitry and Sasha been as perplexed about them as I had?

Those questions were never answered. The American team members continued to speculate about the two men. Regardless of their motives, the performance of our companions was truly impressive. They carried crude backpacks loaded with nearly a hundred pounds of supplies, and they skied up to 50 miles a day. Their shelter was a crude nylon tent supplemented by a sheet of clear plastic supported by snow blocks.

By morning weather conditions had improved only slightly, but driven by the demands of our April 1 deadline for reaching Provideniya, where a research team and press corps from the U.S. were to meet us, we decided to press on. We agreed to set out at seven o'clock. At the appointed hour, Cola was still puttering inside the hut while the rest of us were dressed and waiting to go outside the door. He had yet to pack his bag, much less load his sled or harness his dogs. Our offers to help Cola got no response. I appealed to Dmitry. His comments to Cola also went unheeded. Cola simply would not be rushed, just as Robert and Darlene would not be rushed when they had fallen behind during the storm a day before. This was one distinct difference in temperament that we noted between our native and non-native team members. As Dmitry put it, "Life in their villages has never been rushed. Can we expect that a few weeks on this expedition will change them?"

Though our departure was much delayed, we made good progress that morning and stopped for lunch at another cabin along the sea coast. Inside the immaculately kept hut were the belongings of a sea hunter—a pair of glass sun goggles, sealskin floats, a mariner's compass, harpoon handles and a supply of mukluk straw, the feathery grass used for padding and insulation in skin boots. The scene was enchanting. It looked like a still-life painting and gave us a glimpse of the simple, pleasant life that native hunters have in this harsh land. A soft gauze of sunlight filtered through the large frosted windows, warming the room nicely despite the 10 degree temperatures outside. Ginna said that the charm of the cabin and its lovely setting on a bank overlooking a lagoon gave it the feel of a Cape Cod retreat.

The next village, Enmelen, lay a hundred miles due east of us across a large bay. The coastal route around the bay would be at least half again as long. Though the pack ice looked rough, we agreed to cut across the corners of the bay, thus shortening the distance. Soon we were threading our way around and over massive blocks and ridges of ice. I found the change of pace and scenery exhilarating. But others who had not dealt with this terrain before found it frustrating and exhausting. Compounding the difficulties was a resurgence of head winds. Before long we were spread out over a mile across the ice.

By the time we regrouped, we were severely chilled. Dmitry suggested we head toward shore. He was concerned that the winds might break up the ice during the night. A few people headed that direction. Others wandered about looking for a sheltered place among the ice blocks to set camp. Some might have been a bit delirious from the early stages of hypothermia. We had pushed ourselves beyond the threshold.

Many long minutes passed before we came to a consensus, deciding to set camp in the leeward pocket of a pressure ridge. An hour later we were warm and happy inside our tents, but the confusion at day's end concerned me. We had faltered. The situation required quick consensus, but there was none. If we had been in a real crisis, say an encounter with a polar bear or a sudden break-up of the pack ice, lives might have been lost. Our communications difficulties and our numbers made this team unwieldy. I wondered—and worried—how we would complete the most treacherous segment of our route, the crossing of the Bering Strait.

That evening, to allow more time for my scheduled radio contact with Nome, I struck a deal with Alexander. We were to share kitchen duty but agreed that he would look after dinner and I would make breakfast. Russian custom calls for drinking tea or coffee only after the meal is served. But in the morning, I tried the "American plan," serving hot beverages while the porridge cooked. Ginna,who had a hard time staring at a bowl of oatmeal without having downed a stiff cup of coffee, was delighted, but the change of pace left our Soviet teammates surprised and somewhat irritated. We passed it off with a few jokes but I made a note that it's best to abide by local customs.

With a light tail wind, cool clear weather and smoother ice, we hit full stride that day, covering nearly 25 miles before lunch break. Our spirits soared. Dmitry's son Nikita and I pumped along in front, with the mushers who rallied the dogs close upon our heels. In the distance we could clearly see the mountains that marked the position of Enmelen. It appeared we might be able to take a shortcut directly across the bay and shave at least a day from our schedule. "Enmelen tomorrow or bust!" we shouted to those behind us.

But in mid-afternoon our optimism was dashed by ominous signs. The light just above the distant surface had a certain quivering shimmer. A mile distant I noticed a massive block of ice that appeared conspicuously out of place. Huge flocks of seabirds flew overhead. These signs all hinted of open "leads" or breaks in the sea.

Sure enough, as we skied over a ridge our trail ended abruptly. I surveyed the scene. To the right the lead opened into the waters of the Bering Sea. The large block I had noticed earlier proved to be a massive iceberg that was floating placidly in the ocean. To the left, the wedge of open water continued on toward shore. Worse yet, the ice between us and shore was active. A web of fresh cracks stretched in every direction.

No discussion was needed this time. We all knew we needed to hightail it to shore. We clambered over the rough terrain, knowing we had a few miles to go with just a couple of hours of light. Some of the ice plates were shifting and heaving as we crossed over them.

At nightfall, totally spent, we arrived on shore. Tempers were thin. More than a few barbed comments in various languages were heard in camp that night.

Our route the next morning paralleled the shoreline and took us past the end of the lead. With the safety of land nearby, the lead was now more a thing of beauty than a threat. Seals scampered among the azure ice blocks that lined the edge. The water was bronzed by a paper-thin layer of young ice that had formed overnight. Blue-gray sea smoke curled above the sea in the distance.

By mid-afternoon we reached the shoreline cliffs. On the narrow beachhead at the base of the cliffs a whale jawbone, sculpted by the winds, protruded from the sand. The ends towered high above us. "This must be an elder's grave," said

Ernie as his anthropological interests went to work. He marveled at the size of the jawbone, estimating the whale to have been more than a hundred feet long.

Farther along, on a narrow shelf of land above the beach, we found stone rings that marked the old village site. Circular depressions 12 feet across indicated where each *yarangi*, or skin dwelling, had been. Whale ribs—some still evident—had formed a domed frame over which caribou hides were stretched. Stones had anchored the skins around the perimeter. The entry tunnel and round opening on top had been closed with whale shoulder blades. A hollowed stone with a bit of moss for a wick had been filled with seal oil and had burned night and day.

Ernie guessed that this site had been abandoned well within the last century because moss had not yet carpeted all of the stones and whale bones strewn among the dwelling sites.

Though the inhabitants were most likely Yupik Eskimo, they could also have been Chukchi. Certain families among the reindeer herders adopted the Eskimo maritime lifestyle. I imagined the hunters climbing the high cliffs directly behind the settlement, a perfect vista for spotting the flukes and fins of their prey cutting through the surf. Then they'd scramble down to the shore and launch their walrus-hide boats with paddles flashing and harpoons in hand.

The night brought heartbreaking news from the outside world. On our radio we learned of the Exxon Valdez oil spill in Prince William Sound, Alaska. "Ten million gallons," Ginna repeated time and again in disbelief as the tragic details were radioed to us.

The next day our moods were much brighter. We were about to reach Enmelen, our fourth village. It had been seven days since we left Konergino.

We arrived in Enmelen to a warm welcome late in the afternoon. This Chukchi settlement, cradled in a valley that spills out into the sea, was a lovely place. That evening, we premiered an addition to our community program. Our team sang our version of "May There Always Be Sunshine"—a traditional Russian peace song—in both English and Russian. We modified the words so that it became a song about friendship between Alaskans and Chukotkans. The crowd cheered with delight.

News had traveled down the coast from Konergino of how popular discos were with our team; so Enmelen hosted one as well. Robert served as disc jockey while villagers and adventurers rocked to the beat of Aretha Franklin, Billy Joel and the ever popular Springsteen.

Robert and Darlene proved to be popular, too, among the Chukotkans. Awaiting them in each village was a stack of letters and phone messages from friends they'd made at previous stops.

Word was out that Robert was a highly eligible bachelor. He was thronged by young women at the discos. He certainly didn't mind that. I remembered his remark to a reporter who interviewed him during our trip preparations. Asked how the opening of the border might affect his village's traditional subsistence lifestyle, Robert responded, "Well, we could once again go into Soviet waters to chase walrus and whales and seals . . . ." Then, after pausing while one of his mile-wide smiles took shape, he added, ". . . and girls."

We often joked about romances developing between our unmarried team members and townspeople, but when relations between our team members took that turn, it became a source of concern for Dmitry and me. That was the case with Ginna and Sasha. They had become virtually inseparable. I was torn. On the one hand, their warm friendship provided enviable support for them on the trail, and their relationship was a fascinating example of Soviet-American cooperation.

On the other hand, the relationship was raising eyebrows among team members and villagers. Rumors were filtering back to me that the situation was viewed by some as inappropriate. Dmitry was as concerned as I was. Ginna's and Sasha's relationship was their own business, but we feared it would reflect on the integrity of the project. Dmitry and I concluded that it was time to deal with the relationship. We agreed that over the course of the next week we would find an appropriate time to discuss this delicate issue separately with each of them.

Before leaving Enmelen I spent time with the director of the school, who gave me a outline of the settlement's history. The site, noted as a center for the development of Chukchi culture, has been occupied for thousands of years. The coastline rarely freezes here, allowing year-round sea hunting. Tradition holds that the Chukchi who established other settlements had dispersed from this place.

The Russians who organized the village school and collective farm didn't arrive here until after the turn of the century. Skin-covered yarangis could still be seen interspersed among the small clapboard homes built by the Russians until the early 1950s. The population now includes 295 Chukchi, 94 Soviets and 13 Eskimos.

The school director said he was one of the few men to fill an administrative position in this town. The mayor, the postmaster and the directors of the hospital and collective farm were all women. "Men here value hunting and herding," the school director said to me. "They do not consider administrative work to fit their calling. And," he added with a smile, "women are considered more intelligent on these matters."

The collective farm in this community includes five enterprises. The most important is the reindeer herd. Five brigades of Chukchi herders look after some 10,000 animals.

The second-ranking industry is the fur farm. Some 200 female polar foxes form the basis of this enterprise, which sends hundreds of pelts to the Leningrad fur market each year.

Enmelen also has a brigade of hunters who harvest the town's annual quota of seal, walrus and sea lion. The director told me that the quotas are established on a sustainable basis. Enmelen, for example, has a quota of 476 walrus each year. Families consume much of this meat. I gathered that a large portion is also used to feed the polar foxes that are raised for fur.

The collective farm's two other activities include a small fishing fleet and a sewing shop, where skin clothing is produced. That clothing includes fox hats, caribou parkas and walrus-hide boots.

As in other towns along the route, the reindeer brigades face a labor shortage. More and more Chukchi are finding community life more satisfying than life on the trail for months away from their families. Specially designed mobile dwelling units are being used now to create a sense of community on the trail. A unit consists of a dozen trailer homes mounted on skis. Some of the homes are for families, others are for bachelors or unmarried women.

Two units serve as a common kitchen and recreation hall, complete with television and movie projector. A small diesel generator powers the trailers. They can be pulled in trainlike fashion to follow the migrations of the caribou.

The next village, Nunligran, was just a day's travel away through mountain passes. Chukchi hunters on snow machines agreed to show us the way.

To get to the trail, we had to double back on a narrow track notched into a steep mountainside. That stretch of trail had given us no trouble on our way into town but on the way out we met near tragedy. I was halfway up the steep rise, looking over the edge—gaping at the sheer drop to the sea ice hundreds of feet below—when I noticed two tiny figures in blue Thermax suits walking along the base of the cliff.

I called out to Dmitry, who was just ahead of me, and we raced ahead to join the others and find out what had happened. Zoya was stunned with fear.

"What happened?" I asked.

Between sobs, she told us the story.

Cola had been driving his team up the narrow trail. His lead dog, John Kennedy, was distracted by a bird and turned and darted off the cliff edge, dragging the team and sled behind him. Cola hung on for the wild ride as the sled tumbled down a ravine.

Fortunately a cornice of snow broke his fall and prevented him and his dogs from crashing on down the hill.

Somehow Cola managed to turn the dogs around and drive them back up onto the ledge, thrashing John Kennedy soundly all the way with a ski pole. Once back on top, Cola set the brake and proceeded to mete out punishment to the culprit who had nearly cost him his life.

To escape Cola's wrath, John Kennedy and the other dogs bolted again, yanking the brake loose. This time the dogs shot out over an edge, where there was nothing to slow their fall.

They tumbled pell-mell out of sight. Cola, nursing a smashed nose and bruised pride, could only stay at the top and watch them disappear. An eerie silence followed. Then Cola and Vadim slid down to the shore through the ravine to find what was left of their dog team.

We all waited anxiously for them to return. About a half-hour later Vadim trudged up the trail and reappeared with one of our trip's most memorable comments:

"Cola great stunt driver."

Miraculously the dogs had survived the fall without injury. A while later Cola rejoined us. He was shaken, but his team was in firm control.

On the rest of the way to Nunligran, we wound ever higher through mountain passes. Caribou grazed on the steep walls on either side of us. The animals, perched at different levels against the featureless white backdrop, looked as if they were floating in space. When we reached the top, we looked down a steep, ice-glazed chute.

"Now the fun begins!" I yelled back to the others. The snow machines that had helped tow some of our skiers to the top shifted into low gear for braking action. Down we went.

Those of us on skis rocketed along in tuck positions like skiers on a giant slalom course. The mushers, hooting and hollering, rode their brakes tight to keep from overtaking the dogs as their sleds wove back and forth down the chute.

"I feel like an arctic cowboy at the rodeo," an exhilarated Lonnie hollered over to me. "This has got to be the finest day of my life!" That meant a lot, coming from a man who is perpetually having a good time.

We reached Nunligran after nightfall, catching the villagers by surprise. Nevertheless, children immediately appeared from everywhere to help us tether our dogs and unload our sleds. The children led us to our quarters, a dormitory in a boarding school.

The schools in small Chukotkan villages have only primary grades. Often they have only three "forms," as they're called. Children in forms four and up go to boarding schools in central

COLA
'Great stunt driver'

villages. The school children in this boarding school were home with their parents for two weeks on midwinter holiday.

Our room had more than 20 beds. Gaily painted posters adorned the walls, and a few rows of colored lights twinkled from the ceiling. The pillars along the wall, painted white and speckled in black to look like birch trees, hinted that at least some of the children who attended this school came from more southerly parts of the Soviet Union.

We enjoyed the luxury of a layover day in Nunligran, which allowed time for rest and socializing. Ginna and I met with members of *Eyeck*, meaning "seal oil lamp," a circle of elder Chukchi women who serve as preservers of their native culture. Though native languages are still spoken in the homes and taught in the schools, the women told us of their vigilance to ensure that Chukchi values are not eroded by the dominance of Russian culture. For example, native festivals are carefully maintained. One marked nearly every month. In January, they celebrate the Holiday of the Sun; in February the Holiday of the Moon; in May the Reindeer Birthing Festival; in August the Young Reindeer Festival (the appointed time for marriages, the women noted); and in December, the Reindeer Harvest Festival.

Chukchi have a profound attachment to the tundra. While all of them now have homes in the villages, they continue to spend their summers in yarangis—now mostly made of canvas— among the caribou herds.

I asked about stories of contact between this village and Alaska. Oh yes, said the women, Chukchi often went to Alaska by skin boat and dog sled in the old days. Later, when American sailing ships plied these waters, Chukchi were hired as sailors.

A ship still visits this village. Every 10 days in the summer, the *Chukotka Coastline* brings supplies from Vladivostok to all the villages along our route. In the winter, supplies arrive by helicopter from the regional center of Provideniya, 80 miles down the coast.

Our community program that evening was an especially lively, upbeat affair. An eclectic ensemble of Slavic Russians in Western dress and natives in colorful parkas and skin clothing crammed into the town's small auditorium. After a series of dances by natives of all ages, a Chukchi woman with a guitar took the stage. Her nervous concentration indicated she was about to deliver something she had worked on for a long time. It turned out to be several verses of "We Shall Overcome" sung in passable English. Then, to wild applause from the audience, our team joined her on stage and, arm in arm, sang it with her. I wasn't quite sure how a protest song fit the spirit of the moment, but it was clear that sharing that song helped overcome any barrier between us and the audience.

Then the crowd sat wide-eyed with curiosity as our team unfolded stories of our travels. The program's highlight was a conversation Darlene had in Yupik from the stage with a villager seated in the back of the auditorium. The crowd was amazed to see the language link in operation.

The audience was equally amazed when we added a new component to our community program. Robert and Zoya, who both perform with their village dance companies, had found by then that they had some dances in common. These had been passed down for centuries on both sides of the Strait.

Together Zoya and Robert prepared a dance for our program. Zoya sang and beat her skin drum while Robert danced. It was a big hit. The audience demanded an encore.

The community topped off the evening with a disco. Flashing colored lights and a revolving mirrored ball transformed the auditorium into a dance hall. Robert took his place on stage as disc jockey, helping two Chukchi teen-agers make alternating selections of American and Soviet dance music while villagers, both teen-agers and adults, danced with some of our team members. In the seats at the back of the auditorium onlookers thumped their knees and nodded their heads in time to the music. One Chukchi elder, who looked as if he had just stepped in from a hunt on the tundra, was dressed head to toe in furs. As the room steadily grew warmer, I wondered how he survived.

The dancing took place in groups rather than couples. I danced with three young Chukchi women. In the lobby, Vadim was challenging—and beating—local pros at ping-pong. Adults served tea and chocolates in a side room. When I slipped in there I found our trail companion Slava playing the guitar, captivating a circle of young people with ballads and light-hearted folk songs. All of the youngsters, their eyes glistening with tears, sang along on one mournful ballad. That song, I later learned, was about the pointless loss of Russian lives in the Afghan war.

Slava sang with such feeling that I didn't need to understand the words to be moved by his song.

I asked him that night how he had learned so many songs.

"Me, guitar, vodka and friends every Friday night," Slava responded.

At a quarter past midnight the chaperones announced the last dance, but the dancers prevailed upon them to extend the event for another hour. I danced across the floor and allowed the tensions of the trail to melt away.

When we moved back onto the trail the next morning, Cola had a sled full of his dancing partners. They and two mushers with dog teams accompanied us for a few miles.

Sasha and I skied together, discussing the differences in temperament between native and non-native people. I told him about the practice in psychology of identifying people as Type A or Type B personalities, the former being habitually more driven and the latter more passive. Native people of the north, I observed, would probably all be classified as Type B.

"Yes, and you," he said laughing, "must be a Triple A."

For our camp dinner that evening, we enjoyed a bounty provided by the villagers of Nunligran—smoked salmon, fresh bread and reindeer. Twilight was lingering longer now as we neared the endless sunlight of the arctic summer. The air was calm and the tundra was bathed in pale orange light.

This evening I had to have a chat with Ginna. It was time to talk with her about her relationship with Sasha.

Being frank about a personal issue with a team member is

one of the hardest jobs for an expedition leader. It's risky business. If it causes offense, it can disrupt team dynamics. Ginna and I had a good working relationship, an established pattern of being straightforward with each other. Nonetheless I entered this conversation with much trepidation.

"I have learned to trust your judgment in everything, so I hesitate to even bring up this topic," I said to her. "But it's clear to all of us that your fine friendship with Sasha is being tugged by the allure of romance. My concern is that this might affect our expedition's integrity." I explained to her that already team members and villagers had commented to me about this. "I'm not about to tell you how to run your personal life," I added, "I just want you to be aware of these concerns. I mean, I know we're out here to set an example of Soviet-American cooperation but . . ."

She thought for awhile and then responded, "I don't know what I will do about this, but because you have brought it up, I will do something. I just need more time to think all this through."

We discussed it further but came to no firm resolution.

While planning the expedition, I had thought through the code of behavior for team members. Unfortunately the possibility of a romance on the expedition had never occurred to me. Suggesting that someone agree not to fall in love is pointless, but at least we would have grounds for discussing the issue if a romance developed. "Next time," I thought to myself, "I won't overlook that issue."

One issue I hadn't ignored was the possibility that our visits to the villages would give team members and villagers an excuse for partying. If the vodka flowed, our integrity would take a nose dive. Thus I secured from all team members an agreement that we would just say "no thanks" when the toasts were offered.

At points along our trail, a Soviet film producer and his crew visited us. Sometimes he showed up in a village. Other times he came steaming down the trail in a vizdahote to catch footage of us under way.

He was an intense man, always knitting his brow as he attended to his craft with clipped precision. It was hard for me to believe that his film would match his intensity because the camera his crew was using was old and battered. Its gears clanked and clattered every time the film rolled. The recorder he was using seemed to be held together by bits of tape. Dmitry assured me, though, that he had produced some stunning work.

On our second night out from Nunligran, the producer and his company joined us at our camp by vizdahote. A native man in skin clothing had accompanied them. I watched as they unloaded several wooden shipping crates from the back of their vehicle. Then they proceeded to drive back and forth over them, reducing the crates to splinters. Noting my puzzlement, the producer turned to me and said, "Fire."

How nice, I thought. We'll enjoy our first campfire tonight.

After dinner, the film crew doused the pile of splinters with fuel. Meanwhile the producer and our team member Vadim were busy applying smudges of paint to the native man's face. The producer looked toward me and said, "Shaman." I began to get the picture. They were staging a native ceremony for the camera.

With the fire lit, the native man began dancing around the flames, beating a skin drum and chanting. One of the crew flashed a sheet of red plastic across a floodlight to enhance the visual effect of the fire. Meanwhile, the producer attempted to get our team members to join the "Shaman" in his dance. No one was willing. Robert and Darlene walked away in disgust, saying that this was a cheap exploitation of native traditions.

The producer grew impatient with the dancer, complaining that he wasn't dramatic enough. He danced alongside him, kicking his knees high in the air. The dancer's chants had an increasingly angry edge to them. It looked as if the situation might deteriorate into a fireside brawl. Fortunately, the battery-powered lights grew dim, and the fire burned out. Soon we were all left there, standing in the dark.

The only pleasant part of the event was the smell of the wood smoke. It was a wonderful reminder of my home in the forest, thousands of miles away.

The official response to the queries I made in various villages about shamanism, once a key part of Chukchi and Eskimo culture, was that it is no longer practiced. Villagers point with pride to the fact that clinics and health care professionals have replaced the shaman's role in medicine. But what about the shaman's role as spiritual mentor? It was not evident what, if anything, has replaced that. Religion certainly hasn't. No church exists in Chukotka. The missionaries' zeal that profoundly affected life in the Canadian and Alaskan far north never reached this region. The Soviet system and atheism were imposed on Chukotka in the 1920s.

In terms of the cultural connection between Alaska and Chukotka, our next village, Sireniki, was one of the most important on our route.

Many of the Yupik Eskimo families there have some blood tie with the people of Darlene's home on St. Lawrence Island, Alaska. The miles of Bering Sea that separate the two were traditionally a highway for skin boat travel. When Alaska was purchased from Russia in 1867 and borderlines were drawn, though, the Siberian Yupik people of St. Lawrence and Sireniki found themselves separated by citizenship.

As we approached Sireniki we noticed another change those international differences had created. High on a hillside at the edge of the settlement were the massive red and white radar screens of a military listening post aimed at Alaska. Only in Konergino had we not seen any indication of the military.

Sireniki is in a lovely setting—a gentle hillside along the coast between two massive systems of sea cliffs. As we arrived, several hundred Eskimos in colorful costumes gathered to greet us in the town square. Darlene was embraced by dozens of them like a long lost daughter.

As a gift to our team, the elders presented me with a small wooden model of the slender lashed frame of a skin boat.

A woman in the crowd was holding an infant dressed in a one-piece caribou skin jumpsuit. He was so cute I could hardly take my eyes off him. Noting my interest, she passed him over to me. I got one quick hug out of him, but then when I tried a few phrases of baby talk in English, he became alarmed and squirmed away.

While we were organizing our gear in the school gymnasium that afternoon, Robert came up to me and exclaimed, "They've got skin boats down by the shore that are just like the ones at home! They are coming in from the sea right now. You've got to come see them. It's just like home."

That was becoming a regular refrain for him lately. I was happy to hear it. Earlier in the trek, he had suffered some serious bouts of homesickness. Occasionally he'd hinted that he wanted to quit. But now the familiarities he was finding in these villages were becoming more and more exciting for him.

Robert headed back to the waterfront. A while later Dmitry and I followed him. Robert was helping a group of hunters carry an overturned skin boat—or baidar—from the shore up to storage racks. The eight boats on the racks, all virtually identical, were about 25 feet long and 6 feet wide. They were tapered at both ends and had nearly flat bottoms and gracefully curving side walls. They reminded me of the huge birchbark canoes in which French *voyageurs* once plied the waters of the U.S.-Canadian boundary lakes near my home.

The frame consisted of hefty hand-hewn wooden poles and ribs lashed together with leather strips. Three sections of walrus hide, neatly stitched together with an overlap seam, had been stretched taut around the frame and laced to the gunwales. A motor mount—a wooden box with an open well below it—was just rear of center. Several long slender wooden oars were tucked in between the frame pieces.

A Slavic Russian in business attire stepped up and introduced himself as one of the officials with the village's collective farm. I did my best to translate as he asked Robert in Russian how these boats compared with ones in Alaska.

"They are just like the ones back home," Robert answered, "except we say *umiak* instead of *baidar*." The only design differences he could see were that these had a beefier frame than the ones his village uses and the hulls all had a heavy coat of paint, a practice not common in Alaska.

The man explained with obvious pride that Sireniki makes the best baidars in Chukotka. In fact, the boat builders are establishing a little factory to supply the needs of other sea hunting settlements. Would there be a market for these boats in Alaska? he asked.

I wondered how with my feeble grasp of Russian I could explain to him the intricacies of the Marine Mammal Protection

Act, the federal law that since 1972 has prohibited the importing of any marine mammal products into the U. S. The law's intent is to protect domestic markets of such items as ivory carvings and sealskin clothing for Alaskan natives. It seemed a shame to me that now, as cultural relations are reopening between Alaskan and Chukotkan villages, the law is preventing Soviet and American Eskimos from reestablishing some of their traditional trading practices. I did my best to explain to the man that marketing these baidars in Alaska would be illegal. "But," I added, "someday the law might change."

"I hope so," he responded, adding that his village was already involved in some international trade. As evidence he showed us a shed where Japanese-made outboard motors used to power the baidars were mounted on racks. Nearly all the motors were 40-horsepower Suzukis.

He strolled over with us to where the hunters were cleaning their catch. The sea hadn't yielded much that day—only three small seals and a couple of eider ducks. A man wearing blood-spattered hip boots and a leather apron was stacking the cuts of meat in neat piles on the snow. Women with mesh sacks filed by, making their selections and taking them over to a scale to be priced. The hottest-selling item seemed to be squiggly piles of entrails.

"They'll dry those, salt them and cut them into chips," Robert said. "It's just delicious. Something like Doritos."

I like most native foods, but I winced at the thought of this one.

In a small wooden warehouse nearby, the reserves from more productive hunts were stored. Dozens of seal and several quartered sections of walrus were stacked like cordwood along the wall. In the corners, plump frozen black ducks were piled like cannon balls. The pungent odor of seal oil, like a powerfully concentrated dose of the smell of the sea, nearly overwhelmed me.

Our friend the collective farm official laughed at my reaction to the smell and indicated he had another interesting aroma for us to sample.

He led us up the hill, past the town's tiny coal-fired power plant to what looked like, smelled like and, yes, was—much to my amazement—a cattle barn. As we stepped through a small wooden door, it felt as if we stepped into another world.

We entered a scene far more reminiscent of central Wisconsin than of an Eskimo settlement along an arctic coastline. Our senses were greeted by the smell of damp hay and the lowing of cattle.

As our eyes adjusted to the dim light, we saw two women in long dresses and white aprons tending a dozen cattle tethered in stalls along one wall. Along another wall were pens made of white pickets. The pens held several calves.

A young man in denim coveralls was sweeping manure into troughs in the concrete floor. He greeted us and led us into the back room where a magnificent bull was kept. This was the young man's pride and joy. From the bull's gleaming coat and manicured pen, it was apparent that this animal got lots of special care.

A woman was perched on a stool alongside a cow and was stripping milk by hand into a large steel bucket. Robert watched with amazement. It was the first time he had seen such an operation. The woman and a helper strained the milk by pouring it through a mat of cheesecloth. Then they brought out glasses so we could sample the product. Robert and I each took a long draught of the warm, thick and slightly sweet milk. We laughed at our white mustaches. It seemed impossible that we could sample something so farm fresh in such a remote and untillable place.

Prompted by our delight, the women poured us another glass. And yet another. And another still. Robert and I were too polite to say *nyet*. Before we left—bloated—they saw to it that we had drained their steel milk bucket.

We waddled back to the center of town to join our teammates for our community program. The dancing that opened the event was the most exquisite we had yet seen. With graceful and rhythmic movements, the dancers pantomimed the playful antics of a seal, the sewing of a skin garment and the paddling in pursuit of a whale. The oldest dancers had traditional facial tattoos: two straight lines on the nose and forehead and several circular lines on the cheek. The tattoos were applied with a needle and fine thread rubbed in soot or gunpowder and drawn through the skin. The tattoos were believed to provide a magical defense against evil. The practice is no longer common.

I sat fidgeting in my chair. Tonight I was determined to give my little speech in Russian. At all the other programs we had relied on an interpreter the town had provided—generally a teacher—or one of our Muscovite team members to get our message across. A lot was being lost in translation. I felt that speaking in Russian would indicate to the village the serious commitment we had made to the task of building the bridge. Finally, I knew it would be gratifying for me, a milestone in my effort to learn the language.

I didn't tackle this task on my own. As I skied with my "language instructor," Nikita, the past few days, I gave him lines from my speech in English. He translated them while I transcribed his spoken Russian phonetically. Basically I'd be delivering my speech by rote memory rather than from any clear understanding of its construction in Russian.

In any case, it worked. I rattled off my three-minute speech to the crowd. I spoke about my family and our home in the woods back in Minnesota. I explained that our expedition was intended as an example of Soviets and Americans sharing challenges to reach common goals. Nikita needed to give me only a few whispered prompts. The audience responded with loud applause. It was gratifying to have communicated with them directly.

One special feature of these village visits was that they offered Dmitry and me a chance to have breakfast meetings so we could discuss leadership issues. Unfortunately the topic up for discussion during our breakfast in Sireniki was a difficult one—Sasha's and Ginna's relationship.

I told Dmitry that I had talked with Ginna about our concerns.

Dmitry responded that he had not yet had time to speak with Sasha. Then he explained that he was uncomfortable about doing so. "For many years Sasha has helped me on my expeditions," he said. "But now he wants to be his own man. He becomes very angry if I talk about his activities."

"I understand," I said, "but this matter reflects on all of us."

For me the issue centered on whether their relationship would surface as gossip about escapades among our team members.

Dmitry shared my concerns, along with another one. If Sasha became attached to Ginna, would he return home from Alaska? If not, Dmitry would have to answer for this to government officials in Moscow.

I wanted to be happy for Ginna and Sasha and the fact that this cross-cultural match seemed to be working just fine, but there were too many complications, too many ways that the situation could reflect negatively on our leadership. It seemed irresponsible to ignore it.

A tight trail schedule faced us that day. We had a five o'clock date with the outside world. Minnesota television reporter Jason Davis and videographer Ian Logan, who were covering our trek for *National Geographic Explorer* and for an ABC affiliate in the Midwest, were scheduled to meet us near Provideniya to film our arrival in that port city.

Because we had nearly 30 miles to go, Dmitry had arranged for a fleet of snow machines and drivers—native hunters who intimately knew the complex network of mountain valleys we were traveling through—to speed us along our way.

The Soviet snow machine is made in Moscow. Its trade name is *Booran*—which translates to "Blizzard." A far cry from the sleek, speedy American snowmobile, the Soviet machine is slow and noisy. It is also, however, faster than skiers and dog sledders. I regretted the fact that the exigencies of our schedule required increasing reliance on the noisy and disruptive snow machines.

Unfortunately the machines also proved to be dangerous that day. As we clipped along the tundra in the late afternoon, Ernie took a nasty spill while towing on skis behind one of the machines. As he lay there, it appeared that we had a severe injury on our hands. But a short time later Ernie got up and hobbled around. The fall caused him a great deal of pain and slowed him down for a week but resulted in no permanent damage.

Our drivers dropped us off on a high shelf of land about eight miles from Provideniya. A steep, mile-long ravine took us down to our rendezvous point, a mountain-ringed bay from where we could see the outskirts of the city.

Jason and Ian were nowhere in sight. I wondered if an important media connection was about to go awry. We waited for more than an hour and then decided it was time to move on. We knew the townspeople were awaiting us.

As we skirted the shore of a steep bluff across the bay we got our first look at the city. Despite its setting in a narrow, mountainous, fiord-like bay, Provideniya was far from picturesque. A smudge of brown and gray factories lined the shore. Many of these, we learned, were associated with the town's main industry, the production of prefabricated concrete slabs. The one patch of color, a huge colorful mural on the side of a tall brick building, proclaimed "Provideniya, Port of the Arctic." Along the wharf, shipping derricks towered over a rusting fleet of harbor boats.

A collection of skiers, snow machine riders and people on foot came out to escort us into town. Along with them came a man driving a homemade contraption on three big bouncy balloon tires.

We organized ourselves in our "parade formation." Cola's sled, out in front, towed our flag bearers, Ernie and Alexander. Dmitry and I skied directly behind the sled. The other skiers followed in pairs with dog teams interspersed among them.

A cheering throng lined our route, which wound for several blocks on narrow streets lined with tall buildings. At the city center we found ourselves enveloped in a tumultuous crowd. Some 2,000 people, we later learned, had waited several hours in the 15-degree weather to greet us. City officials offered words of welcome on a bullhorn. Then we were swept along to the sports hall, a brand new building with three floors of meeting rooms and a large gymnasium with well-equipped locker rooms.

A few hours later, the downcast TV crew of Jason and Ian walked in. They had a sad story. Their vizdahote driver had taken them to the wrong rendezvous point. When they realized the error and tried to turn around, the machine became stuck in waist-deep slush. While we were enjoying a spectacular and highly photogenic welcome, our reporter and videographer were trudging some two miles back to town. In his dour mood, the best Jason could come up with to replace the fine news story he had missed was a cynical piece on the alleged infallibility of vizdahotes.

What made the situation even more unfortunate was that I sensed Jason's frustration was creating a negative cast to his stories. This concerned me greatly because his news reports from the trail would be the first to reach viewers in the States. The first reports were sure to leave strong impressions.

When I asked Jason about my concerns, he assured me his coverage would be fair. But I should have taken seriously the telling little quip he added with a laugh. "Don't worry," he said, "good news doesn't sell anyways."

My concerns were justified. I would later learn that his story that made the biggest splash was billed as *Conflict Between Soviet and American Team Members.*

We spent our first morning in Provideniya undergoing more fitness tests. The team of Soviet doctors who had gathered data in Anadyr joined us. They were joined by three American researchers who arrived on the charter plane that had brought Jason and Ian from Nome, Alaska.

We also had a little time to tour the town. The 5,000 people who live here provide administrative services for the eastern half of Chukotka. Provideniya is a major port and is visited by hundreds of Soviet ships each summer. A collective farm on the edge of town provides fresh vegetables and milk year-round.

The stores carry a limited range of goods that were very expensive. Dresses, for example, cost at least $60 and a TV set carried a $1,000 price tag. The housing is a series of long concrete apartment complexes. Rent is heavily subsidized and runs about five percent of a family's income. Salaries average $1,200 a month, nearly three times the standard wage in Moscow. The subsidy is part of the Soviet incentive system for encouraging the development of remote regions.

Later that afternoon we presented our community program in the civic auditorium. It proved to be a sophisticated affair.

As Dmitry said to the crowd, the beautiful furnishings of the auditorium, the formal, banner-draped stage and the fine clothing of the audience made us feel very much as if we were in Moscow.

That urban atmosphere was evident again that evening at our dinner party at the city's main restaurant. Our hosts, wearing evening dresses and suits, introduced themselves as the founding members of the city's new Club for the Development of International Contacts. The group had formed in response to the "Friendship Flight," the one-day goodwill visit of some 70 Americans to Provideniya that had taken place the previous June courtesy of Alaska Airlines.

The restaurant was decorated with Soviet and American flags and banners. Fresh carnations adorned the tables. Also provided were plenty of bottles of beer and vodka. For our convenience, most of these had already been opened. It was obvious that the program was going to involve more celebration than business.

Sasha and I were seated at a table with a young couple and two older women. While Sasha spoke with the couple, I talked ever so slowly with one of the women in English—she knew a few words—and with the other in German, dredging up what I had learned in high school.

A waitress came by with glasses for beer and vodka. Sasha glanced up at me with his sly smile, wondering how I would handle this challenge to our ban on drinking. I looked around the room and, noting that other team members were having no trouble suspending that rule for the evening, I decided to do the same.

On my earlier trips to Moscow I had learned that certain of my Soviet friends take mischievous pleasure in the fact that their tolerance for alcohol exceeds that of most Americans. It doesn't take long for the Soviets to drink a Yankee under the table. I had fallen prey to that source of local amusement more than once on my visits to Moscow. I wondered how our unsuspecting American team members would fare tonight.

Soon one toast after another to Soviet-American friendship was being offered up around the room. The pace was picking up. Well before the dinner had been served, celebrants took to the floor for dancing. Waitresses carrying platters of fried chicken fought their way through clusters of dancers in the darkened room. Between dances, I found myself getting swept from table to table as people asked to chat with me. Finally, overcome with hunger, I firmly parked myself at one table and dug into plates of chicken, jellied tongue and peas. The dancing was growing more raucous by the minute. The woman tending the tape deck made sure the music kept pace with the crowd.

The woman next to me, a cheery brunette in her late 30s, was an English teacher. She wanted to talk about glasnost.

"Believe me," I said, "now's the time. We're in the thick of it here." I laughed as I watched one of the visiting American researchers come twirling by in the arms of two young Soviet women.

The teacher explained that the people of her generation have been suspicious of the sweeping changes they've experienced in the past few years. Initially, many people thought the changes were only tricks, deceptions that would lead to new subtle forms of repression. Now, though, the people are convinced that the changes brought about by perestroika and glasnost are for real, and they feel compelled to fight to preserve those changes and seek new ones.

There is one problem, she said. Young people are already beginning to take the changes for granted. As an example she referred to her 11-year-old son. "He does not share my love for perestroika," she said, "because he does not really understand how different things used to be. How can he have any idea of the repressions we experienced?"

She said her goal is to instill appreciation of those changes in her son and her students to help ensure that the next generation of leaders will bring even more progressive ideas.

The party ran on well past the town's midnight curfew. Fortunately the vice mayor was in attendance and announced "martial law," declaring the curfew extended until 1:00 a.m. Our glassy-eyed team, along with the reporters and research crew, joined hands with our hosts and wove a series of galloping snake dances around the restaurant. The Soviet gentleman holding my hand noted wryly that their club's efforts to establish international contacts had been deemed a huge success tonight.

At closing time, the vice mayor cornered me for one last

toast. Did I have any suggestions about how to make the town more appealing to foreign visitors? he asked. "Yes," I answered, "hold more parties like this one and paint colorful murals on the drab industrial buildings along the wharf."

His eyes lit up. "Exactly!" he said. "That is my plan for this summer. Perhaps you can help us get some paint from Alaska."

After leaving the restaurant, most of the party-goers reassembled in various apartments to extend this exercise in glasnost a few more hours. I went back to the sports hall to get some sleep. I found Kosta and Vlodya—our "KGB friends"—in the locker room having tea and cake. They invited me to join them. Sitting cross-legged on gym mats and sharing tea brewed on their campstove, we exchanged what information we could in the few words of Russian and English that we shared.

They told me they had traveled all over Chukotka by ski and kayak as well as on foot. They traced their routes on my map.

I told them I was impressed by their fitness. I was amazed, I said, at their ability to keep up with us on the trail while carrying packs twice as heavy as ours and without the benefit of sled dogs.

They posed the litany of lifestyle questions I had become accustomed to. How much money do I make? How much land do I own? How much did I pay for my car? What caught my attention was the comment they made when I told them I was 33 years old. "Same age as Jesus Christ," they murmured matter-of-factly to each other.

I couldn't believe it. That was fourth time I'd heard that comment in Chukotka. Never had I heard that reference to my age in the States. I never got an explanation for this and was left perplexed as to why the age of Christ has come to be so significant in this supposedly atheistic part of the world.

My cordial conversation with Kosta and Vlodya that night struck another blow to the espionage theory. If it wasn't for the cool reception they had received from our Moscow team members, I would have been ready to dismiss any notions that they were part of a covert operation.

Our demanding schedule and the needs of the media crew intensified the pressures of the next day, Monday, April 3.

As usual, we were trying to pack too much in, and, as usual, the media connection would go haywire. A couple of school functions and meetings with Soviet officials were scheduled in the morning. Then at two in the afternoon, we were to embark for New Chaplino, a small Yupik Eskimo settlement 15 miles to the north.

New Chaplino was a milestone of the expedition, and we had looked forward to it for some time. New Chaplino, like Sireniki, is a center of Yupik culture and has many ties with Darlene's home of Gambell on St. Lawrence Island, Alaska.

Our arrival in New Chaplino would be a momentous event for Darlene, who has many relatives there. We had been alerted that a special Eskimo reception awaited us. We promised to arrive before sundown.

Paul recognized the ancient design of the herder's sled.

Rough terrain slowed sledding to a crawl.

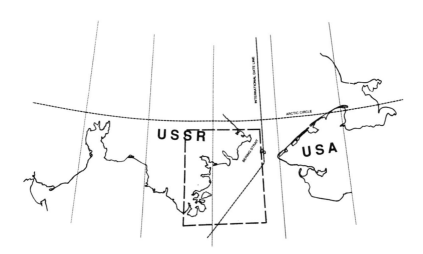

SIX

ШЕСТЬ

Our arrival in New Chaplino was also a key event for reporter Jason Davis. This was his last chance to film such an
event. It was also his only chance to film life in a Soviet Yupik
village. A chartered airplane would be returning our American
visitors to Alaska in the morning. Jason needed a colorful story
to justify the expense his television station had incurred to send
him here. Furthermore, this footage would be a key element of
the documentary *National Geographic* was intending to produce.
It was imperative that we arrive in New Chaplino while there
was still daylight.

Dmitry and I had discussed these concerns in detail over
breakfast. But come two o'clock, while other team members
were loading sleds, Dmitry was nowhere to be found. At half-
past he sauntered in and began packing his bag. As frustrated
as I was, I held my tongue. I realized he had much unfinished
business with local officials regarding logistics and finances.
Unfortunately, these negotiations continued even after I ushered
him outside to join the others, who were waiting for us with
sleds loaded and skis on.

Finally, at 3:30 we embarked, having three hours of travel
ahead of us and just about that much light left in the day. It
was too tight for my comfort, so I set a brisk pace. Fortunately,
the team members were psyched and the sleds were light. The
vizdahotes that transported the press corps also carried much

of our equipment. Jason and Ian, along with a number of other photographers from Chukotka and Moscow, jumped out of the back of their tracked vehicle from time to time to film us on the run.

We hit our halfway point as the sun was about to dip below a razorback chain of mountain peaks. Jason, whose vizdahote had stopped just ahead of us to allow for the "sunset shot," was a bundle of nerves. When a Moscow photographer stepped into Jason's camera view, Jason let loose with a fit of verbal abuse that could have been understood in any language.

Fortunately our approach to the village was a long downhill grade, allowing us to pick up speed. Ahead we could see a large cluster of people forming on the tundra near the village. The vizdahotes raced ahead so the photographers could get their equipment set up.

About a quarter mile from town we stopped to display our flags. Sunlight had been reduced to an orange glow behind the mountains. In the coastal valley where we were, daylight was disappearing fast. Within minutes Jason wouldn't have sufficient light for filming. I could see a large group of dancers in native costume lining up in front of a backdrop of banners. Kids were racing out to meet us.

Just as we got under way toward them, someone in the crowd let off a volley of fireworks. The dogs recoiled in fear, wrapping their harness up in knots. I threw up my arms in despair. We were in for a long delay. After 10 minutes we were still waiting for Cola to get his dogs sorted out. Utterly exasperated, I shouted angrily at him to hurry up. That was pointless and I regretted it. It only served to aggravate him.

By the time we got moving again I could see Jason and Ian walking off toward the vizdahotes with their cameras packed in cases. My heart sank. I tried to console myself that though the filming was over, this would not affect the outpouring of joy from the villagers.

Indeed it didn't. The greeting was moving and breathtakingly beautiful. Darlene was smothered in hugs by relatives laughing, and crying with joy.

Nearby, three generations of colorfully dressed Yupiks—elders in the back, singing and drumming, parents and children

DARLENE
Smothered in hugs

in the front, dancing—expressed through movement and song what they felt in their hearts. The dancing had power, the power of time and traditions that bond a culture together. Knowing the scene wouldn't be captured on film, I studied it intensely, hoping that it might at least be indelibly etched in my memory.

With the dancing over, the crowd swept us along toward the village.

I met Jason on the way and offered my condolences to him about missing the footage. I asked him what he thought of the ceremony. "I didn't see it," he answered. "I was so angry and frustrated, I couldn't bear to watch. That mistake might have cost us the documentary."

I wrestled with his assessment as we moved our gear into the school. It was a bitter pill to swallow. The documentary was important to us as a means of sharing this experiment in Soviet-American relations with a wider audience.

On the other hand, one of the qualities of this expedition that I took great pride in was that its effectiveness—unlike that of our North Pole journey—did not depend on media fanfare. Our goal was to establish direct contact with the thousands of villagers along our route. That was being accomplished regardless of the media's involvement.

I took solace in the fact that we would be on our own again the next day, once we were away from the pressure cooker of outside interests.

Our community program went on until midnight in the village hall. Jason and Ian caught a few minutes of it on film and then raced off into the night by vizdahote to Provideniya.

I sent with them a tape-recorded message for Susan and Bria and all of our exposed still and video film.

From Jason's and Ian's hasty departure, I could tell they were eager to set foot on familiar soil. We were all homesick too, but now that a month had passed, the rhythm of this journey had become a way of life for us. That night I looked around the hall at the smiling faces. Our surroundings seemed natural. The villagers felt like neighbors. Even the beat of the skin drum seemed to be something I had known for a long time.

On stage, two young men portrayed ravens in an exquisite and humorous dance that brought a thunder of applause from the crowd. For how many generations, I wondered, had that raven dance delighted the people of Chukotka? It was this time-less and comfortable quality of the people and their culture that gave this place so much appeal for us.

Our native team members had many invitations to honor that night. They visited from house to house.

In the morning while the rest of us were involved with school programs, Darlene continued catching up on news with her relatives. She returned with cases of gifts for friends and family in St. Lawrence.

About midday we headed on our way. We were destined for Yanrakinot, a small Chukchi village 30 miles ahead.

The day was a harbinger of spring, calm and sunny with temperatures rising just high enough to soften the snow for the first time on our trek. Skate-skiing along, we enjoyed a spectac-ular panorama of ice-glazed mountains along our northward coastal route. It felt great to be steaming along again as an expedition. We were on track to arrive at the Strait in mid-April, barring bad weather. With the harried scheduling pressures of Provideniya and New Chaplino behind us, I wanted nothing more than to settle into a steady rhythm of skiing and sledding. In particular, I was glad to be freed from reliance on snow machines. In fact, I had discussed this with Ginna and Ernie that morning. They had agreed with my proposal that we would decline any further offers from villagers to speed us on our way.

That afternoon we passed along the shores of Aracham-chechan Island. Thousands of walrus haul out on the rocky shores on this spine of land each summer. The ancestors of the people of Yanrakinot once lived there and relied on these animals for sustenance. Now the island is a wildlife preserve, and the villagers live just across on the mainland, where walrus meat only occasionally complements their staple of reindeer.

As the sun began to set, the village of Yanrakinot came into view on the mainland coast, just across from the north end of the island. *Yanrakinot* is a Chukchi word meaning "small hill that stands alone," and it's an apt description. We had but 10 miles to go. In a few hours we'd be there.

Behind us I could hear the drone of a snow machine. Dmitry had mentioned that the Soviet film crew who had filmed us in Provideniya might meet up with us on the trail occasionally during the next few weeks. Looking back, I confirmed that it was the film crew. But to my great disappointment Ginna and Ernie were towing along behind the front machine. "Oh no," I thought, "We're in for a confrontation."

When they pulled up beside me, Ernie responded to my look of disappointment by saying, "Well, there's no danger. The machines are going slow."

"But you agreed with me that we wouldn't rely on these anymore," I countered.

As we debated, Dmitry, Alexander and Sasha pulled up in tow behind a second snow machine. Joining the argument, Alexander offered his rationale. "Paul, the importance of this expedition is not our sports record but our diplomacy, our visits in the villages. With help from snow machines we can have more time in the villages."

"Agreed," I said, "but when the snow machines are being used only to spare our team members some work, it's a cop-out."

Dmitry entered in, applying all the charm he could muster. Smiling warmly and wrapping his arm around my shoulder, he said, "Paul, you are a great idealist. If you say no snow machines, we will not use them. But I think Alexander is right. Our sports record does not have great importance. For us, snow machines are OK."

The discussion continued with no one speaking up to support my position. I began to feel like a badgering moralist. It appeared that the use of snow machines was a compromise I would have to accept. I didn't mind compromising on matters of leadership style or cultural differences, like what order we ate breakfast in or which dog team led us into the villages. I did mind compromises that reflected on the integrity of the project. This, I felt, was one of those. It remained a festering issue throughout our trek.

We pulled into Yanrakinot at nightfall. Chukchi villagers, many in caribou parkas, gathered for an impromptu welcoming ceremony. In their midst was a striking red-haired woman in an elegant wool coat and fur hat. She introduced herself as the mayor and presented us with a loaf of bread and a short speech about how our journey served as evidence that perestroika and glasnost were reaching the most remote corners of their country. Dmitry and I were intrigued to know that this woman was managing a settlement of Chukchi reindeer herders and walrus hunters.

In the morning she joined us for breakfast at the village's tiny restaurant, a low plastered hut with eight small tables. She said she had moved here from the Ukraine a couple of years ago. I asked how she felt administering one of the most remote and impoverished villages in her country.

"Yes, we have problems," she answered through Dmitry. "But these are our challenges. We are very simple people here, but good people. I like my job very much."

Later in the day we took a tour. First we stopped at the school. The children, nearly all Chukchi, attend three forms. Their older brothers and sisters attend a boarding school in New Chaplino. "But this is very difficult for the families and older children," said one teacher. "We hope very much to have a complete school here some day."

The children were playing with dolls, trucks, games and building blocks in a colorfully decorated rumpus room. Against the wall were two televisions, stacked one on the other. Do the children watch much television? I asked. "Not much," a teacher answered. "We receive few programs here. But the televisions do make a very good place to put things," she added with a laugh, as she pointed to the dolls perched on top of them.

We all gathered in the classroom. Alphabet charts in both

Chukchi and Russian were on the wall. The teacher handed us a globe as we attempted to explain to the children where we lived. They understood Alaska all right, but this place called Minnesota was definitely a new concept for them. Fortunately, the Mississippi brought smiles of recognition. It was the only topographical feature of the U.S. on the globe. It was marked as a wide blue line that neatly bisected the U.S. from top to bottom. It seemed no wonder that the books of Mark Twain were so popular throughout the Soviet Union.

After saying goodbye to the children, I asked our escort, a Chukchi man who served as the mayor's assistant, if Sasha and I could visit a typical village home. "Certainly. Which one?" he asked, sweeping his arm past the 30 or 40 tiny homes with white plaster walls and plank roofs that made up the settlement. I pointed to the nearest one.

He led us in through a lean-to entryway that served as cold storage. Stubby oval snowshoes, seal skins stretched taut across a plank to dry, braided leather lassos and partially assembled caribou garments hung on hooks near the door. A middle-aged Chukchi woman in a knit red sweater and black skirt greeted us warmly and invited us in.

Inside were two small rooms, a kitchen and living area, heated by a coal-fired brick cookstove. On the floor in front of the stove lay the caribou hide the woman had been scraping when we arrived. Nearby stood a steel drum filled with water and a stand holding a metal wash basin. A hindquarter of caribou lay thawing on newspapers in the corner. An electric light bulb dangled from the ceiling. On the wall above a small wooden table was a large picture of Lenin surrounded by faded family photographs.

The woman led us into the other room to introduce us to her mother, who was blind and bedridden. Her mother's name was Toina. She was 85 years old and spoke only Chukchi. Our escort, who translated her comments into Russian, explained that the older Chukchi were never given Russian family names. On the old woman's bedstead hung her personal possessions—a tobacco pouch, a skinning knife and a sewing kit, all made from hide or bone and richly decorated with beadwork and tufts of fur.

When I introduced myself as being from the United States, a bright smile broke across her face and she attempted to sit up. Yes, she said as she reached out for me to hold her hand, she had heard of Alaska, but she didn't know anything about the place. She had never traveled beyond this village or the surrounding tundra. She listened with interest as I told her that many Eskimo lived there but no Chukchi. "Very glad to meet you," she said over and over again in Chukchi as we said good-bye.

The village had no plumbing. One central outhouse—a six-holer—served the village's 500 residents. There was also a small *banya*, much like a Finnish sauna, which some of our team members had enjoyed the night before. Behind the community center where we stayed, a building was being erected —"the first to go up in many decades," the mayor had told us. The walls were stacks of squared timbers like rail ties pinned together with huge steel spikes. With a coat of plaster inside and out, it would be ready for its residents as a four-plex.

During our noon-hour community program, the villagers surprised Cola with a special gift—an affectionate young sled dog. They had learned that a dog awaiting Cola at a village farther up the trail had died. He had hoped to add that one to his team for our travels in Alaska. This one was offered as a replacement. He beamed with thanks but decided to leave it behind because he felt it was too young to handle the rigors of the trail.

This village had many teams which, by all accounts, included some of the best working dogs on the south coast of Chukotka. Judging from the motley mix of dogs we saw tethered on overhead chains behind many of the homes in the settlement, though, some control on breeding was sorely needed. Although we'd been told that specimens of the original blue-eyed Siberian husky could be found in Chukotka, we never saw any. The dogs we saw were clearly well trained, and they were excellent performers, but they were inconsistent in physique, coat and size. They weren't purebreds. Villagers told us that although the dogs we were looking for still existed, they were with the reindeer herding brigades in the interior of Chukotka.

During our mid-afternoon lunch that day we made plans to

travel on several miles toward Lorino while our good weather held. A front moving in from the south suggested a change.

The plan, though, did not sit well with Zoya, our doctor. It was the first time I had seen her upset with me. According to her assessment, Dmitry and Alexander needed more rest. "We stay one more day," she insisted. I pointed out to her that we'd all found our nights to be more restful on the trail than in the villages, but she was adamant. "Must here stay," she repeated to me in the English she had learned in the past weeks.

I presented the issue to Alexander, who was standing nearby. He said he did feel tired but was ready to continue traveling. Later I discussed it with Dmitry. He agreed that more time in the village would do him good. He needed the rest and wanted to meet with regional officials. We agreed that the team would continue on toward Lorino and that he would catch up with us on a snow machine the next day. Off we went with a rather glum Zoya, who was upset that her authority as team doctor had been challenged.

I wanted to support her in that role. She took her responsibility seriously and was doing an excellent job.

In fact, at our community programs Ernie often told how impressed he was with her skills. He explained that she had prescribed treatment for the leg injury he sustained when he took the spill behind the snow machine as we approached Provideniya. While in that city, he sought second opinions from two visiting American doctors, who were there as part of a research effort. Their opinions concurred exactly with Zoya's, said Ernie.

That evening we reached a hunters' cabin 15 miles north of Yanrakinot. The cabin was tiny, and only a few of us could sleep in its fetid confines, ripe with the smell of the last hunt, so we also put up our tents.

Our wake-up time was set for 7:00 a.m. But due to some confusion with our watches, the team was rousted at 6:48— minutes early. Under normal circumstances such an annoyance would go unnoticed. But for us and the fragile dynamics of our team, it became a major issue.

The mistake proved most offensive to Alexander. With his background as an electronics technician, he had a fetish for precision; he and I went head to head about who was to blame for awhile and then dropped it unresolved. I thought nothing more of it, but it left him a bit shaken. He decided to stay behind that day and wait for Dmitry to come by on a snow machine while the rest of us continued on our way.

The trail and weather conditions were superb. Our team, reduced for the day to 10 people, clipped along at its fastest pace ever.

I passed the time chatting with Ginna. Both of us come from large families—my parents had six children and hers had five—and we shared thoughts on the transition our parents had gone through when the nest emptied.

We also talked about our religious beliefs. She and I are both Christians. Only two others on our team ever expressed an interest in church. Ernie is a Quaker, and Alexander worships with Christians in Moscow.

Then Sasha joined our conversation and the topic turned to the Bolshevik Revolution and the history of Soviet society. Sasha is dismayed at how much of the history of the Stalin era was rewritten to cast a favorable light on that horrible regime. The truth may never be known, he said, because many key documents were destroyed.

Time and miles passed quickly, with good conversation, and by lunchtime we found ourselves 25 miles along, sharing lunch with an Eskimo hunter in his hut. His transistor radio was tuned to an Alaskan station, KOTZ in Kotzebue, Ernie's hometown. The hunter couldn't understand English but indicated that he liked the country-western music on that station. Ernie listened with keen interest as the day's birthday wishes were read over the air to his hometown friends and neighbors. An update came on about the oil spill in Prince William Sound. We learned that the disaster was even greater than we had thought.

On our way out the door, we examined the hunter's factory-made wooden skis. Extremely wide and more rounded than pointed on the ends, they looked very much like water skis. Vadim explained that their width allowed the hunter to ski on top of the powdery snow that sometimes blankets the tundra.

Throughout the afternoon we cruised down the coastline at a refreshingly brisk pace. Ernie, the human skiing machine,

ERNIE
Human skiing machine

joyfully pumped along, steadily gaining distance on the rest of us. Though days before we had agreed to stay closer together, I found it hard to bring myself to tell him to slow down. I knew how exhilarating it was to hit full stride on skis and hold it all day long, the body fully engaged by healthful activity and the mind engaged by the expansive beauty of the arctic.

As I watched him breeze along, disappearing and reappearing as a tiny black speck among the rolling hills miles ahead, I thought about what makes expeditions so appealing for me.

It's the all-consuming nature of the challenge, the fact that expeditions like this one demand that I operate at capacity—not just physically, but mentally and emotionally as well—for days on end. Adventuring offers a sense of life in "fast forward." Heightened experiences and sensations are packed into a relatively short period of time. Expeditions serve as a concentrated source of personal growth.

My thoughts were interrupted when we came upon a couple of unattended track vehicles at the top of a hill. Their load was a massive steel tube with a circular stairway welded around the outside. I thought I'd have some fun with it.

"Look, Ginna," I said as she joined me on the hilltop, "a nuclear missile silo."

"Oh my God," she answered, aghast. "What an awful thing to run into out here."

Then Lonnie joined us and I got him going on the same line. Soon Vadim arrived and found the three of us gawking at the structure. "What's the matter?" he asked.

"Nuclear missile silo," said Ginna pointing, "Very bad."

Vadim laughed and laughed. "No missile silo," he answered and said that it was a tower for a coastal navigation beacon.

It was clear he was right, but it was the closest we came to seeing anything that resembled a strategic weapon in Chukotka. If any were hidden out there in the vast expanse of tundra and mountains, the locals I asked indicated they had no knowledge of them. Considering how well they knew every subtle feature of the land, I doubt that anything could be hidden from them.

In the evening the weather thickened and our route took us along a sand spit between the sea and a large lagoon. The spit was pockmarked with depressions of now-gone yarangis that marked an ancient village site. Whale rib bones with holes bored in them at various heights protruded from the dunes in orderly rows like some Eskimo Stonehenge.

Checking our maps, we found we had but 10 miles to go to reach Lorino.

The prospect of clocking our first 50-mile day excited us, and it amazed Dmitry and Alexander, who soon arrived on snow machines. They hadn't expected us to reach this village today. We moved on and soon reached Lorino.

As we had done in Yanrakinot, we caught the villagers in Lorino unawares, and they scrambled to greet us and arrange accommodations. Nonetheless it was obvious that they were happy to see us.

In the crowd were several faces familiar to Dmitry, Sasha and me. This village and the next one, Lavrentiya, were the communities we had visited briefly the previous November during our planning. I thought of the dinner of Russian and Eskimo delicacies we had been served in the town hall.

I remembered when our hosts pointed out the window toward Alaska—whose mountains peaks easily can be seen from here on a clear day—and talked of the times when skin boats regularly plied the waters of the Strait during the summer. They spoke of the boatloads of Alaskans who, decades ago, came over each year for their Eskimo games festival and competed with the Chukotkans in such events as high-jumping over dog sleds, lassoing reindeer antlers and racing up hillsides while juggling sticks.

I especially remembered their answer to my question about whether they would like to see all that happen again. The answer, interpreted via three languages, was that they were "burning" to do so.

Now three months later I was back with them. As we unloaded our sleds in front of the school, the people who had shared those stories came up and embraced me like an old friend.

We spread out our equipment in the school gymnasium. The four-story brick school was new and well-appointed. In fact, it was one of the first buildings we'd visited in Chukotka that wouldn't have looked out of place in an American community. Lorino was obviously a prosperous place. We made plans to spend a layover day here and I looked forward to having time to learn more about this community.

That evening while I was hanging dog harnesses to dry in the gym, Robert came bounding up to me, radiating one of his million-dollar smiles. Close behind him was an older man. "Paul, I'd like you to meet my relative," Robert said. He could hardly contain his excitement. This was the first relative he'd met in Chukotka. Robert explained that as soon as he mentioned to the villagers that his last name was Soolook, they ran off to find the local clan connected to that name. Robert found that he and his relatives shared enough words of the Inupiaq Eskimo dialect that they could communicate a bit. He let me know that we probably wouldn't be seeing much of him during our stay in Lorino. "I have visiting to do," he said with joy.

That same evening misfortune struck. A distraught villager came running into the gym gesturing frantically toward the school yard. Lonnie and I gathered that a dogfight was under way. Lonnie raced out the door. A few minutes later he returned. "I'm afraid I have very bad news," he said.

Cola's stakeout chain had broken and his dogs had jumped one of ours, the lead dog, Kohojotak. "I don't think he's going to make it," Lonnie said.

Bracing myself for the worst, I followed him outside. Lying in the snow, Kohojotak was listless and whimpering softly. Multiple puncture wounds had left his once-beautiful white coat matted with saliva and blood. Internal damage was evident. His abdominal wall ballooned in and out as he struggled to breathe. We were anguished to see one of our most spirited dogs in such agony, and we felt helpless. Our veterinary first aid kit was well-stocked but it was no match for the serious injuries we faced here. We carried the dog inside and placed him in the corner of the school's entryway.

Amazingly, a veterinarian who looks after the village's reindeer herd and fox farm happened to be in town. The villagers summoned him for us. After examining Kohojotak, he said the external wounds were not serious, but he also said that only major surgery would save Kohojotak if his digestive tract had been punctured. The presence of blood in the dog's next stool would tell us whether there was internal damage. The vet suggested we wait until morning before doing anything.

We got little sleep that night. At daybreak we hurried downstairs, hoping for a miracle, but Kohojotak was barely alive. His eyes were rolled back in his head and his breathing was labored.

Our breakfast in the school cafeteria was a somber affair. Mournful cries from Kohojotak echoed through the building. It sounded as if he were gasping for life. "This is more than I can bear," Lonnie said as he stepped away from the table. "I can't stand to see him in such pain. It's obvious he won't make it. Let's put him out of his misery."

Again Lonnie summoned the vet, who this time brought a gun and a sled for carrying Kohojotak out of town. But he also brought some consolation. The villagers felt so bad for us, he said, that they had offered to give us the dog of our choice from their teams to replace Kohojotak. We were grateful for that generous offer but were deeply saddened at the thought of losing a dog we had come to know.

We headed downstairs to tend to Kohojotak, but I just couldn't bring myself to do it. Lonnie and I discussed it again and decided we'd load the dog up with antibiotics and sedatives and wait a little longer. Maybe we could still hope for a miracle. The vet agreed to keep him over at his clinic. Now all we could do was wait. The full schedule of activities the villagers had planned for us that day managed to keep our minds off our worries about Kohojotak.

Several of us visited with the workers at the village's fox farm. Here we learned why Lorino is so prosperous. The furs produced here for the Leningrad Fur Market are the envy of Chukotka. Each year this settlement exceeds its production quota. The fur farm isn't the villagers' only thriving enterprise. Chickens—some 50,000 of them—are also raised here to provide meat and eggs for the region.

The 30 or so workers we spoke with were comprised of a roughly equal mix of Chukchi, Eskimo and Slavic Russians. I sensed great rapport. They showed much pride in their work. By the standards of a free-enterprise economy, their fox and chicken farms would probably not be considered profitable. The difficulties of distributing products from such a remote place would surely preclude that.

It was clear, though, that the fox and chicken farms provided something far more important to them than profit—meaningful work for many villagers and a source of identity and cohesion for the community.

The workers spoke of their keen interest in learning more about how American business operates. They felt they could learn much from us about creating incentives for increasing worker productivity.

I responded that we could learn much from them about how employment can be provided in remote northern settlements through economic activities like animal husbandry, in which the Chukotkans have excelled. I was particularly intrigued with their success with collectives—state-owned farms that provide a salary for the workers and operating funds for the community.

The notion of communally owned property is a traditional element of northern culture. Perhaps that is why the organization of collective farms has been so readily embraced by the Chukchi and Eskimo of Chukotka. I wondered if native Alaska settlements might also benefit from more collectives.

Later, Ginna and I pondered the fascinating socio-economic experiment that's likely to occur as communication opens between the Soviet and American settlements of the Bering Region. The resulting free flow of ideas will surely benefit both sides of the Strait. We considered that what might be most useful at this point would be an exchange of researchers who would study and compare the economic and cultural elements—both positive and negative—of the villages in both countries. We looked forward to sharing these thoughts with our contacts in Alaska.

A community leader in Lorino told us that this village, like others in Chukotka, still relies on some subsidies from the federal government. He added that the dependence lessens each year. He thought it was reasonable to expect that someday the village would become a net producer rather than net consumer. "That is our goal," he said. "We all have much hope for that."

The townspeople had a special treat in store for us that afternoon. They transported us by vizdahotes several miles up into the mountains to the local "hot spot," a series of geothermal springs. Here, clean 180-degree water bubbles up from a fault zone and fills three natural pools. Around the pools was a small complex of buildings, including greenhouses, a small lodge and dressing rooms.

The presence of a wind generator on a tower indicated that some effort was being made to find an alternative for the throbbing diesel engine that powered the buildings and disrupted the relaxing atmosphere.

Wearing suits borrowed from the lodge, we frolicked in the largest of the steaming hot pools, burrowing our sore feet into the near-scalding sand, pitching snowballs at each other from the drifts that lined the shores and circling up in the chest-deep water for team back rubs. We were giddy with laughter and felt like kids. This was glorious, the most fun we'd had yet as a team.

Some people from the village enjoyed the pool with us. So did three regional officials who had arranged for our visit here. They told us of their interest in building an international-class hotel here as a means of bringing hard currency into Chukotka.

Although talk of a hotel might have been dreamy speculation, I was impressed by the itinerary for tourist trips that they had worked out. The program, involving a three- to four-day regional tour, would include trout and salmon fishing, a visit to a reindeer herders' camp, rides on reindeer sleighs and dog sleds and an evening of entertainment by native dancers and Eskimo athletes as well as visits to the hot springs and nearby settlements.

We explained to them that their proposal was similar to tours already available in Alaskan villages. But, we added, theirs would offer tourists the undeniably enticing appeal of a visit to Siberia. And it might well be an exciting component to add to the "Circle Arctic Tours" that have become popular in Alaska. When it came time to return to Lorino, the officials were brimming with excitement.

Our evening was especially festive. The native dances, outdoors against the backdrop of the setting sun, were spectacular. The community program was a spirited event with much banter between team and audience. And the disco was jammed with villagers of all ages.

The next morning as we packed our sleds, the moment of truth arrived—it was time to check on Kohojotak. Mustering up our courage, Lonnie and I trudged across the village to the tiny clinic behind the fox farm. We approached the building quietly as so as not to disturb Kohojotak. I went to reach for the door but then jumped back with a start. There he was, a curled clump of white fur, lying in a hollow of snow near the door stoop. He was motionless. We called his name softly. For a second I assumed the worst, but then he lifted his head. I called his name again. He wagged his tail feebly and sat up.

"I think he's going to make it," I said as I exchanged smiles with Lonnie. We helped him to his feet. It took him a few clumsy steps to gain his balance but then he followed us with a slow, measured stride.

Lonnie made a nest for the dog in the back of his sled. Townspeople and our team were elated at the dog's recovery as we left town. By the time we reached Alaska, Kohojotak was ready to pull again.

A few miles northward along our route from Lorino, Ginna, Sasha and I made a short detour with our Soviet film crew to witness a caribou roundup. Out on a tundra plateau, we found a Chukchi brigade tending several hundred animals that had been herded into a wooden corral. Caribou galloped round and round in a tight circle, churning up a cloud of snow and dust with their hooves. Chukchi men and women wielding large

123

sheets of canvas as movable fencing diverted a few animals at a time into a chute. They selected the breeding females to be released to fresh pastures with little snow and protection from the spring winds.

As the caribou raced out of the chute onto open ground, other herders lassoed them. Once the animals were roped, a group of teen-aged boys tackled them to the ground. Some of the animals were branded with irons dipped in cans of yellow paint. Others were dehorned or castrated. These jobs were performed by the elders.

The rhythmic pounding of hooves mixed with the joyous cheers and howls of the herders. All of the duties were performed with a measure of bravado. Obviously this event was as much ritual and sport as it was work.

Alongside the corral, grandparents watched children at play while mothers stirred cauldrons of caribou stew suspended from tripods over wood fires. Cuts of meat were being selected from a caribou that had been neatly disassembled and laid out across the snow like the pieces of a puzzle.

Many women were dressed in richly decorated ceremonial skin clothing. One woman, for example, wore a knee-length coat that was a striking mosaic of colored furs.

It was the perfect weather for a winter picnic on the tundra—calm and clear with a temperature in the 20s.

The roundup struck me as cultural communion, a means by which the Chukchi share in the body and soul of the animal that has virtually defined their race. From birth to death, their lives are linked with the caribou. Chukchi babies are ushered into the world swaddled in caribou hides. Often the Chukchi dead are buried on the tundra under a hide anchored with stones. The number of antlers heaped on the grave reflects the herder's status.

Perhaps only the North American Indian tribes who once followed the herds of bison that blanketed the Great Plains knew such a visceral attachment to a single animal. I wondered if the Chukchi's profound association with the caribou made their world more comprehensible to them than ours is to us.

Lonnie agonized over Kohojotak's wounds.

From the tundra, a surprise—a three-wheel Tin Lizzie.

Chukotkan photographer K. Lemeshev asked the team to accept these four photographs, which show "our life as we see it."

A herder and his dog outside his yarangi.

Herders face harsh conditions on the tundra.

Life inside the yarangi has warm moments.

Life on the tundra—the herd, the dogs and the people.

SEVEN

СЕМЬ

That afternoon we headed for Lavrentiya, a large town 25 miles to the northeast. Lavrentiya sits 85 miles due west from the tip of Alaska. We were near the narrowest point of the Strait.

Lavrentiya is Zoya's home, and a tumultuous welcome awaited her. We approached the town down a long sweeping hill. Dozens of people, mostly children on skis, made their way up the slope to greet us. Among them was Zoya's husband, a short, stocky Slavic Russian who works as a government administrator. He greeted his wife with a polite hug and a red carnation. Then her nine-year-old son stepped forward and was engulfed in hugs from Mom.

We paraded through town to the cheers of hundreds of people who lined the streets. At the village square we gathered around a massive pink granite bust of Lenin.

Dmitry and I were presented with flowers to lay on the base of the monument. Dmitry had been alerted to these plans in Lorino. He had asked me that morning if I would be willing to take part in such a ceremony. I had wavered on the request. I felt terribly uncomfortable about seeming to endorse a man whose politics I don't accept.

Finally I agreed to Dmitry's request, reasoning that it wasn't as if I would be pledging allegiance to the Soviet flag. It was just a gesture of respect for a nation's former leader. Dmitry had shown the same respect when we had visited the monuments

in Washington, D.C., in January, when we held a press conference.

After the ceremony the crowd shifted its attention from the
monument to the steps of the auditorium. An Eskimo dance
performance was under way. Conspicuous among the dancers,
all wearing native dress, was one in a bright blue wind jacket
and pants. Her zest and radiance outshone them all. It was
Zoya.

Tears of joy rolled down her cheeks. Robert and Darlene
joined her for the final numbers as our other team members
pressed their way closer to the dance floor to share this moment
with them.

What a remarkable woman Zoya is—a mother of four, a
pediatrician, an accomplished native dancer and now a proven
adventurer and dearly loved member of our team. I laughed
when I thought of the doubts I'd had upon first meeting her in
Anadyr. She didn't strike me then as someone who could mush
along hundreds of miles of arctic coastline. How delightful it
was to have been proven so wonderfully wrong!

Zoya's homecoming celebration continued on through the
evening. Native villagers prepared a feast of Eskimo food for us.
The meal included tundra greens, which tasted much like let-
tuce, along with muktuk, seal and walrus.

Then the villagers invited us to join them for a demonstration of Eskimo games. The first was a Eskimo version of arm
wrestling, in which opponents lock their fingers and try to yank
each other off balance while seated cross-legged on the floor.
Lonnie took on the town champ—and nearly got his arm yanked
off in the process.

Then several of us tried our luck at the high kick, attempting
to touch with our toes a ball suspended directly above us.
Alexander excelled at it.

A third event was the long jump, in which the jumper
launches from a squatting position. It looked easy. The native
athletes soared with seemingly little effort. But I could barely
gain a couple of feet on my two attempts.

In the morning, our team members trooped off to various
schools to meet with students. Dmitry and I had spoken at one
of the schools when we visited here in November. Since then,

ZOYA
Doctor and dancer

the teachers and students had been hard at work on a geography curriculum about the U.S. Their efforts included preparing albums of news clips about U.S. events and painting posters on Soviet-American friendship in the Bering Region. The walls were lined with displays of Soviet-American study projects.

That afternoon Dmitry and I had an appointment at the barbershop. While a young woman washed and clipped my unkempt mat of hair, I fell sound asleep. Minutes later I awoke to find my hair cut in the distinctive style I'd seen throughout the Soviet Union—sides trimmed short with only a slight taper, and crown left long. I was taken aback but then I began to like the look. "I guess my transition must now be complete," I joked to my barber. "I am a new Soviet man." The tip I offered her was refused.

Zoya and her family hosted us for dinner in her home, a neatly decorated three-room flat. Wearing a white silken blouse and dark blue skirt, she scurried about carrying a variety of Russian and Eskimo foods to the table with help from her husband, son and daughter. She was chatting happily to her daughter and it was obvious that she had made the temporary transformation back to being a wife and mother with aplomb.

The size and furnishings of flats are more or less standard throughout the Soviet Union. Zoya's flat looked similar to ones I'd seen elsewhere in Chukotka and in Moscow. Floor space including closet and bathroom was about 300 square feet, a bit larger than the average American living room.

Furnishings are designed to make the most of a small space. In the kitchen, a large wooden panel that is pulled down from the wall over the sink provides counter space. Pull-out beds turn the dining room and living room into bedrooms. A huge bureau that extends the length of the dining room wall includes cupboards for dishes and linens, drawers for clothing, bookshelves and a glass china cabinet. Despite tight quarters, Soviet homes don't look crowded. The families maintain few possessions and these are always neatly organized and displayed.

The possessions in Zoya's home included a concertina, a television and books—lots of books. Soviets are avid readers. On Zoya's shelves were the complete works of Lenin, a collection I'd seen in virtually every office and home I'd visited. Alongside were Russian editions of various American authors, including Twain and Hemingway. In the china cabinet was a beautiful display of glassware and ivory carvings. The piece that particularly intrigued me was an old ivory pipe with delicate etchings of a seal-hunting scene on the side. Noticing my interest, Zoya's husband removed it from the cabinet for me to look at. He explained that it had been given to him by an Eskimo hunter who, he thought, had found it among diggings at an old Eskimo village site. "Please take it," he said handing it to me. I was deeply moved by this wonderful gift and had little to offer in return except a pin with a Soviet and an American flag. He was pleased with this and proudly put it on his lapel.

A phone call interrupted our dinner chatter. Zoya answered and then handed the phone to me. "USA," she said with a look of bewilderment. I pressed the receiver to my ear. Through the crackly static on lines that stretched all the way back to Minnesota, I could faintly hear my wife's voice. "It's Suzie!" I shouted to the team members huddled around me. I could hardly contain my excitement. This was our first contact in nearly a month and a half.

We shouted back and forth for half an hour, giving no mind to the $200 phone bill we were racking up. The news from home was all reasonably good, except that the expedition bank account was overdrawn, sponsorship checks had been delayed and our new batch of sled dog puppies had clawed their way out of the pen and were chewing up everything in reach around our home. I felt terrible that Susan was stuck with all these hassles, but she seemed to be tolerating them fairly well. On top of it all, she was now four months pregnant, but she was doing great, or at least she made it sound that way.

"How did you ever track us down by telephone?" I asked. She explained that, having learned of our whereabouts from a phone message I'd left in Alaska that morning, she had been trying for more than four hours to reach us.

Fortunately the international operator in the U.S. was sympathetic and had stuck with her throughout the day. When they finally got through to Moscow, the Soviet operator was stumped. She had no idea where Lavrentiya, Chukotka, was.

The Soviet operator offered to call back the U.S. operator after she got a map of her country and figured out how to route the call. Thirty minutes later, Susan's phone rang with the Lavrentiya operator on the line. Susan mentioned my name. The operator knew through the grapevine, as did the other 4,000 residents of Lavrentiya, that our team could have been found at Zoya's that evening.

After dinner, Lonnie and I accepted an invitation to join a group of teen-agers at the music club. We listened to voice and piano performances of classical, rock and folk music.

In return, Lonnie sang the one country-western song he knew: "T is for Thelma." I strummed a few bluegrass tunes on a guitar. I was impressed to learn that these young people got together most evenings as their principal means of entertainment. They were exceptionally talented, and their repertoire seemed endless.

One of their songs was another ballad about bloodshed in Afghanistan. A girl translated the words of a verse for me:

> We can't forget the mountains of Afghanistan.
> Someone's lying there on the ground.
> Look at him girls. Look at him boys.
> This is the face of a man who is twenty and who will be
> twenty forever.
> We can't forget the faces of dying friends.
> Sometimes I think they will return.
> Someday they will return.
> We will remember the names of those who have died.

Many of the youngsters spoke of their plans to go away to college in the next year or two. Few expected to return. One girl answered that though she loved her hometown, she felt she could "serve her country" better elsewhere.

The phrase caught my ear. I had heard it often in the Soviet Union. Although Americans tend to use that phrase only in reference to military service, Soviets often associate the word service with their careers. I found this sense of comradeship and service to country to be strong in the Soviet Union. The people seem genuinely concerned about the nation's common welfare.

Early the next morning Cola realized that one of his dogs was missing. It had gone on a "walkabout." Days later we would be crushed to learn that the dog had met up with a bullet by following his curiosity too close to the fox farm, where roaming dogs are shot on sight.

Meanwhile, as our futile search for the dog carried on, a crowd grew. About 200 young skiers gathered around us. The day had been declared a school holiday to honor our departure.

Among the crowd was a little guy named Misha. He was about 10 years old and had been my near-constant companion during our stay in Lavrentiya.

Following me everywhere I went, he pointed out the sights of his village and chattered away in Russian about his friends and school. He never quite comprehended that I couldn't understand most of what he said to me. But I enjoyed his company and his cheery smile. Wearing slender wooden skis more than twice as long as he was, Misha managed to ski with me about three miles out across the bay as our entourage got under way. I dreaded having to say goodbye to him. Suddenly he spun his skis around and headed back, nodding goodbye with such nonchalance that I wondered if he assumed I'd be back the next day. "He is young," commented an older boy skiing nearby who knew some English. "He does not understand where you came from or where you are going."

The snow machine issue came up again. As we made our way across the bay, I looked back and was astonished to find Dmitry towing behind a machine. When he came by me, I asked, "How can you feel right about towing when all these school children are skiing alongside us?"

He agreed to ski, but that lasted only awhile.

In the afternoon, long after the school children had turned back, he approached me to say that the hut we would camp near that night was a long ways off. He and Alexander would go ahead by snow machine with our film crew to set camp and prepare dinner so those tasks wouldn't have to be done in the dark. I wasn't pleased. It struck me as an excuse for laziness, and I felt he was reneging on our agreement not to use snow machines any more.

As Dmitry and Alexander raced ahead with a machine, the rest of us continued along by ski and sled. We organized ourselves with fast skiers breaking trail in front and weaker skiers in back, where they could get help by holding on to the sleds from time to time. Despite the hilly terrain we made steady progress. At the top of one rise we looked down over a beautiful pink and gold sunset panorama. It was nearly eight o'clock, time for our radio contact with Alaska. Camp was yet an hour ahead. Because we were approaching our last village before crossing the Bering Strait, it was crucial that we stay in close touch with Anne Walker about the schedule. To stop now and set up our antenna on the tundra would mean getting into camp well after dark.

I was in a quandary. The film crew, having dropped off Dmitry and Alexander at camp, had circled back to film us skiing through the sunset. They could give me a quick lift so that I could set up our radio closer to camp, but since I'd taken a strong stand on that issue, some of the team members might see this as a glaring contradiction. I decided the radio call and our evening schedule were more important than my pride so I took the lift.

This decision came back to haunt me sooner than I expected. While studying our maps in the tent that evening, I overheard Sasha point out to Dmitry on the map where I had caught a ride on the snow machine. They both chuckled, assuming I couldn't understand their conversation in Russian. It was time, I knew, to bring the issue to a head.

Over breakfast the next morning I opened a meeting for a general airing of grievances. Complaints flew. We debated our agreements concerning the snow machines and the tightness of our schedule. Nothing was resolved. But then none of the issues really mattered. None of them would make or break our expedition, and none of them could be defined in black and white. All were gray.

The problem was that, given our limited shared vocabulary, issues we discussed as a team almost always came out sounding as if one side of the argument was dead wrong and the other totally right.

Often team members aligned as Americans versus Soviets. We didn't like doing that. In fact, we tried desperately to avoid that. After all, we were determined as a 12-person team to set a good example of Soviet-American cooperation. But often communication limits and, sometimes, cultural differences, stood between us and our goals.

When we couldn't understand exactly what the Soviets' feelings were, we were left with a choice. We could either say to ourselves, "I don't know quite what they mean, but I'm going to give them the benefit of doubt and assume they are well intended." Or we could just as easily say to ourselves, "They are dead wrong on this issue and being total jerks about it." If we were in a good mood we'd choose the former.

On this morning I was not in a good mood. When our sleds were packed I set off from camp convinced that Dmitry was being a total jerk. Fortunately, Ginna noticed my mood. Skiing alongside me, she cautioned that we couldn't afford a disruption in team dynamics now that we were nearing the pivotal point of our trek—the crossing of the Strait. The challenges that lay just ahead required total harmony. She was right, of course. I appreciated her advice. Many times on this journey her insights proved invaluable.

Though she and I remained at odds over her relationship with Sasha, that didn't prevent us from putting our heads together to discuss leadership or logistics. Dmitry often sought her advice as well.

Ginna remained our point person on diplomacy. We learned that the protocol she had helped draft in Anadyr had been approved. Plans were being made for Governor Steve Cowper of Alaska and Governor Vyacheslav Kobetz of Chukotka to meet us at the International Date Line by airlift to sign the document.

We were elated. The agreement called for visa-free travel across the Strait by Bering region natives as well as enhanced trade, transportation and communication across the Bering Strait.

Our crossing of the Bering Strait was to coincide with the signing, now scheduled for April 16. That would give us three days in Uelen, our next—and final—Chukotkan village, to plan and execute a strategy for crossing the Soviet waters of the Strait. We needed to reach Ratmanova, or Big Diomede, as Americans know the Soviet island that lies adjacent to the Date Line, at least the day before the signing event.

Many crossing strategies had been discussed. A few weeks earlier, reconnaissance information we had received from the Soviet border patrol indicated that firm ice existed over the 30 miles of ocean that separated the mainland from Ratmanova. We were ecstatic then. The reports suggested that a surface crossing might be possible. We savored the thought that we could reach Ratmanova by ski and dog sled. Our plan back then was to reach Uelen and wait for a day with a high-pressure system that would promise calm, clear weather over the Strait. Then we'd embark at sunrise on a dash to reach the island before nightfall.

But it proved a fleeting hope. More recent reports indicated that huge gaps were developing in the ice. Expecting a breakup, Dmitry had dispatched a member of his support staff from Anadyr to Uelen to check on the availability of hunting boats we might use to cross the Strait.

The prospect of crossing the ice-choked Strait in small boats was not something I looked forward to. It struck me as more adventure than I had bargained for. Since the project's conception I had known that boats might be necessary, but information gleaned from natives on both sides of the Strait, and satellite images taken of the ice over the past 20 years by weather observers, indicated we had a reasonable chance of finding good ice.

As we approached Uelen, I hoped for a miracle. Just maybe, I thought, we would learn that those gaps had closed. Those hopes were thoroughly shattered that evening.

We reached the town at sunset. After a spirited welcoming ceremony, the villagers escorted us to the school. The windows of the gym on the second floor where we spread out our equipment faced northeastward toward the Arctic Ocean. Bracing myself for the worst, I walked over to the windows to have a look. My heart sank. "Oh no," I said to Lonnie. Open water stretched as far as we could see.

We learned at dinner that evening that the Strait had opened up wide in the past few days. Dmitry's support staff reported that three wooden whale boats were available to transport us, and three of the best native boat captains in Chukotka had been summoned to Uelen to help guide us. They would begin preparing the boats tomorrow. We could expect to depart in a day or two.

The morning brought a change in weather—and a dramatic change in our plans. Instead of the balmy south winds that had blown the coastal waters free of ice during the past week, we now were getting gusts from the northwest. On the northern horizon we could see huge wind-blown blocks of ice creeping down from the polar sea.

Our situation only got worse. Just before noon I was able to get through to Anne back in Nome. "I'm afraid I have lots of bad news," she said. She had learned from the National Weather Service that the storm we were experiencing was forecast to grip western Alaska and the Bering Strait for nearly a week. All airports in the region had been closed. The governor's office had announced that the Soviet-American ceremony on the Date Line had been moved to April 23, Alaska time.

That was nine days away. We would have to decide, Anne said, whether to bide our time in Uelen or continue on our way, perhaps foregoing our participation in the ceremony. Looking out the window at the gale-force blur of snow, I realized the weather would probably make that decision for us.

The weather news was disheartening but nothing compared with the blow that was yet to come. "Paul, I need to speak with Ernie immediately," Anne said.

Ernie took the receiver. His face tensed up in knots as he listened. "Oh no!" he gasped before handing the phone back to me. As he left the room Anne told me that his son, Ernie Jr., 23, had been killed in a car accident the day before. The accident had taken place in Missouri where Ernie's son and his wife lived with their new child. Anne told me to help Ernie place a call to his mother, who was standing by her phone in Kotzebue, Alaska.

I went out to look for Ernie but he couldn't be found. He had taken a walk in the storm to be alone with his thoughts. I passed the news along to the other team members. Early that afternoon we met up with Ernie in the village restaurant. He was subdued but willing to talk about the tragedy. He hadn't seen his son in more than a year but had talked to him by telephone just before leaving on the expedition.

"He told me then that he was proud of me for going on this expedition," Ernie said. "And then he said 'I love you, Dad.' That's all I needed to hear."

I asked if he'd like for us to try to arrange a charter flight to fly him home. No, he said. Considering the weather and the distance to Missouri, he probably wouldn't get there until long after the funeral anyway.

With winds still buffeting us and with the forecast in mind, we settled into Uelen for our long stay and came to know the town well.

The long narrow town was stretched along a spit of land that separated the ocean from a large lagoon. Nearly all the buildings were on a single, mile-long street.

On the east end was a Soviet border patrol station—a fenced compound with a lookout tower and buildings painted in yellow and green camouflage. On the other end of town was a polar research station—a large complex of buildings where scientists and technicians gathered atmospheric data. During our stay they provided us with regular updates on the storm front.

A mix of single-family dwellings and apartment buildings provided housing for Uelen's thousand residents. Among the other buildings were two grocery stores, a hardware store, clothing store, hotel, post office, grade school, high school and community center.

Although most of the buildings were aging wood and stucco structures, the school we stayed in was quite new. The school was made of preformed concrete panels and it had—for Chukotka—a strikingly modern look.

The pride of the town, however, was an older, light green two-story building. This was Masterworks, a studio where the best native artists of the region perfected their talents. The ivory carvings produced here are reputed to be among the best in the world. More than a hundred artists are based at this collective.

The work was exquisite. The sculptured animals were strikingly realistic. Many of the pieces were whole tusks on which had been etched—in scrimshaw fashion—scenes of traditional village life.

As one artist pointed out to me, some of the engravings have been "enriched" by sociopolitical themes. At the Lenin Museum in Moscow, he said, is a tusk devoted to the theme of "Chukchi Legends about Lenin."

Many team members made close friends among the villagers and spent most of their time out visiting. Darlene and Robert found distant relatives and moved into their homes.

Also in Uelen we said goodbye to our "KGB friends." They planned to continue on skis a hundred miles westward up the coast to reach their homes in the village of Neshkan. They wished us well. I never did find out if they were monitoring our activities in any official capacity, and it probably didn't matter, because they seemed truly fond of us and our project when they left.

I became friends with the English teacher at the school where we stayed and helped with some of her classes. The kids all wore uniforms—blue suit jackets for the boys and brown pinafores with white blouses for the girls. I had a ball, and the kids were excited to have a guest teacher.

"They have never been so attentive," said the teacher, Ludmilla Tachenko. "I don't think they ever really realized before that English was a useful language."

The lessons moved along briskly—none lasted longer than two minutes or so. We worked through telling time, reading a calendar and counting. Between each, the students would take an exercise break in the aisles, doing windmills and jumping jacks in unison. They'd also take turns reading to me from an instruction booklet in English that was organized as a series of questions and answers. The children's pronunciation was good, but I'm not sure how much they comprehended. Some of it was heavy stuff—and it had a twist to it. One question, for example, was, "What do you want to do when you leave school?" The answer: "In the Soviet Union young people have every chance to choose a job for which he or she may be well suited. The situation in capitalist countries where there is always unemployment is very different. It is not easy for young people to find work there. In fact many school-leavers have to join the army of the unemployed."

On one evening, Ludmilla invited me to her home where she lived with her husband, Edward, an artist, and her 12-year-old daughter, Christina. Also sharing their three-room apartment were Torilla, a tortoise; Moorzik, a cat; Seema, a parrot; and a cock and hen named Peyta and Seepa.

Ludmilla had grown up near Moscow and moved here 15 years ago because, as she said, "the remote setting intrigued me." Her husband's father had been born in Manchuria. Edward had grown up in the Soviet Far East and had moved to Uelen to hone his artistic skills at the village's famous studio. Life here suits them just fine, said Ludmilla. "We have more freedom than in Moscow because we are so far away no one cares. This is the most remote village in the Soviet Union. We have a local saying, 'There is no further place they can send us.'

"We get very good wages here. Housing is free for teachers. So we use my salary for living expenses and save Edward's for our vacations," she said.

Residents of the Soviet north also get out every three years. They receive a free pass to fly anywhere they want in the Soviet Union.

"Of course it is sometimes difficult to get things here," Ludmilla said. "At the post office there is a catalog called *Goods by Mail* but the service is notorious. It can take many months for orders to arrive. For special occasions we serve what we call Chukotka Cake made from the few ingredients that are generally available in our store—like flour and concentrated milk. What we can't buy, we make or we try to grow."

Her husband tends the community greenhouse. This winter they had harvested pounds of tomatoes and cucumbers. "We even have tulips blooming now," she said.

I noted the Japanese tape player on their Soviet television

in the tiny living room. "Edward got that through connections," Ludmilla said. "He brought it home with him from a vacation in the west."

A Charlie Chaplin movie was showing on the television as we talked. Today was his 100th birthday and it was being celebrated across the Soviet Union with a film festival.

Later that evening, there was more evidence that Uelen isn't so isolated. Ludmilla's daughter came home from a birthday party. She reported that the gifts her friend received included a Charles Dickens book and *Alice in Wonderland* records.

The residents of Uelen may have the resources to deal with isolation but they do have to cope with the hazard of polar bears. "They come through the village every week," said Ludmilla. "This year they ate some dogs and tried to grab the guard on duty at the polar research station. When bears are spotted all the parents are alerted to bring their children inside. So far," Ludmilla said, "there have been no fatalities."

Those few light moments in Uelen helped relieve my anxieties about our crossing of the Strait.

Plans changed day by day as we monitored the wind and ice conditions. The storm that had greeted us when we arrived in this village continued to rage on our second day. Coastal waters were choked with ice that had been blown in by the north winds. Ice blocks of all sizes paraded along the shore toward the Strait. I wondered how the rapidly changing conditions would complicate our plans.

Dmitry soon answered that question. He had met with our Chukchi boat captains. They had told him that the wooden whale boats were too heavy and unwieldy to maneuver among the ice floes. Unless the waters opened up again, these boats were no longer an option. What was? Dmitry had asked. Our best bet, they said, were baidars, the lightweight walrus-skin boats we had seen in Sireniki.

Unfortunately, baidars are no longer used in Uelen. Villagers told us that the last time an Eskimo boat plied the waters between here and Ratmanova, where a Soviet Eskimo village had been located, was in 1941.

"How could we get a baidar?" Dmitry asked.

"Let's contact that official with the collective farm in Sireniki who was keen on promoting the boats produced there," I suggested. "Perhaps he would like to lay claim to having one of his boats be the first to cross in nearly half a century."

When Dmitry reached the official by phone, the man readily agreed to provide a boat.

Border patrol officials, who had become intrigued with our problem, agreed to pick up the baidar with a military cargo helicopter and deliver it to Uelen. They also agreed to Dmitry's request to take us on a reconnaissance flight over the Strait.

When Tuesday morning brought a break in the weather, we were summoned to the helicopter pad. Three officers in flight suits ushered us into the cargo bay.

I fumbled with my cameras, wondering if I'd be allowed to take pictures. If the Soviet government prohibits photography from passenger aircraft, surely filming border installations from a helicopter is a serious indiscretion, I thought. I decided I'd try. As we became airborne, I raised my camera toward the window to get a shot of the town. The navigator quickly got up from his seat and came toward me. "Goodbye, Nikon," I thought. But instead of taking my camera, the navigator swung a gun turret out of the way and opened the window. Then he motioned for me to lean out and get a better shot. I was awe-struck at yet another example of the openness and hospitality with which the Soviets had treated us all along our route.

The scene below us was overcast but beautiful. Spectacular rugged cliffs plunged sharply down to the sea edge. Shelf ice extended out about a half mile. The ocean beyond to the north was a hodgepodge of large ice pans, jumbled heaps of rubble, patches of mush and expanses of open water. Shadings of blue showing through the fog to the south suggested that more open water might extend in that direction.

It took only 15 minutes to reach Ratmanova. Its sheer walls climbed steeply from the water and disappeared into a cloud bank. We flew low over the border patrol station along the island's north coast. Perched on a finger of rock jutting from a ravine in the cliffs was an octagonal sentry post. Radar and searchlight equipment sprouted from the rooftop. On a ledge in the ravine, a series of buildings surrounded a courtyard. A trail led up to the clifftop where a helicopter pad and radio tower were located.

We cut around the east side of the island, heading up the center of the Strait. The International Date Line, the imaginary global seam that separated me from my homeland, lay somewhere down there on the surface outside of our starboard windows. Through those windows we could see America, or at least a tiny chunk of it. Ratmanova's diminutive twin, Little Diomede Island, rose up from the ice just a little more than a mile away from us.

There at the base of a cliff on Little Diomede's westernmost flank was the cluster of buildings of Robert's hometown, Little Diomede, a village of some 178 Inupiaq Eskimos and a handful of non-natives. Everyone in the helicopter was pointing excitedly toward it. "Hello, USA!" shouted the navigator over the roar of the rotors. He took a photo with his own camera. Then he walked over to me and asked that I autograph its leather case.

From our aerial perspective, it seemed as if we could almost straddle the Date Line—with a foot on each island.

Dmitry studied the little island and broke into laughter. "You mean that is America?" he asked me, shaking his head.

"Yes, it even has a ZIP Code: 99762," I replied with a smile.

The channel between Little and Big Diomede Islands was firmly frozen. Dog sledding across would be no problem. Some of the ice was studded with rubble, but there were many flat spots through the center. That was good because the ceremony marking the signing of the border protocol was to take place down there soon, and the Soviet and American officials would need to be flown in by helicopter.

Looking down again upon the Soviet waters of the Strait as we headed back for Uelen, we saw that open channels to the south offered some hope that we would be able to thread our way toward Ratmanova by baidar. One large crescent-shaped gap spanned most of the distance. It tapered to a close among a mass of large ice pans about five miles from Ratmanova.

Over dinner back in Uelen we discussed what we had seen. If that gap to the south held another day, it might just be our highway. But the last five miles would be a real slog. We'd either have to wedge the ice pans apart with wooden poles and push the boat through them, or heft the boat up onto the pans, rest it on dog sled runners and tow it across. It would be grueling and quite possibly dangerous. If a block flipped or broke and we took a dunking, we'd face hypothermia. The prospect left Dmitry and me uneasy.

This piece was carved in extraordinary detail from an ivory tusk.

Native talents are nurtured in the Masterworks studios.

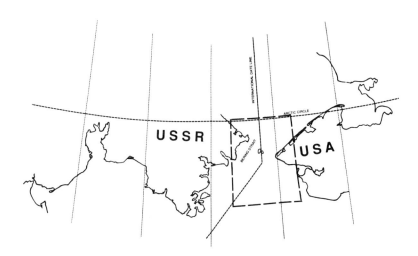

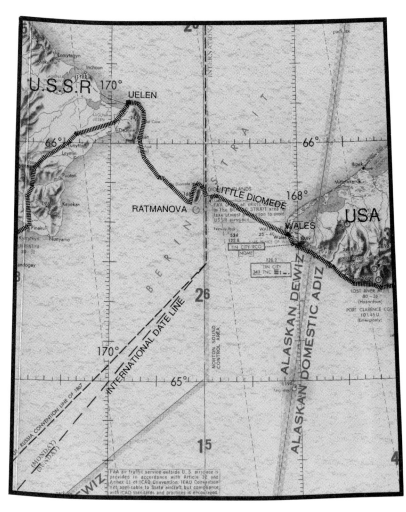

EIGHT

ВОСЕМЬ

The baidar arrived on Tuesday. Emerging with it from the cargo helicopter were our boat captain, Andrei Ankaly, and his assistant, Anatoly Ractilkun. These two Yupik Eskimo hunters would escort us to Ratmanova. Andrei, we learned, had built this graceful 25-foot boat the summer before. Its stout wooden frame—a network of ribs and struts—was securely lashed with wide bands of rawhide strapping. The hides that had been stretched over it and laced in place around the gunwales were nearly as taut as a drumhead. The outside of the hull had a protective coat of yellow marine paint. Inside were long hand-hewn wooden oars, two floats made of seal hides that had been cinched on the ends and inflated, a dozen life vests and knee-high rubber boots. A 40-horse Suzuki motor would fit in the motor well near the rear of the boat. Operating that motor would be Anatoly's job.

Our native team members gave the boat their nod of approval. "It looks seaworthy to me," said Robert. But I still felt uneasy about trusting my fate to this arctic version of an overgrown birchbark canoe. I insisted to Dmitry that we allow time for training with this boat before heading out to sea. It was too late that day to move it out to the sea edge, but Dmitry agreed that we'd make time for practice before it was launched.

As I returned to town, I thought that if we were to make history in this boat it needed some identity. I arranged for

Ludmilla's artist husband to brush *Bering Bridge Expedition,* on the center of the hull, in English on one side and in Russian on the other. Then, near the bow, I had him give the boat a name—*Ernie, Jr.*

As big as this boat was, it couldn't possibly carry 12 team members, two guides, 18 sled dogs and several hundred pounds of supplies and equipment. Our baidar was no ark.

From the time we'd begun considering using a boat we had accepted that much of the load would have to be flown over by helicopter. Most dogs are afraid of open water and would certainly not tolerate a day of bobbing through the waves. And if the dogs were to be shuttled to Ratmanova, team members would have to accompany them.

Andrei, our captain, indicated that 10 people, including himself and his assistant, Anatoly, would be a safe load for this journey. The plan called for Cola, Zoya, Darlene and Robert to accompany the dogs and most of our equipment by helicopter to Ratmanova.

On Wednesday morning the border patrol reported calm clear weather over the Strait and offered to make another run to Ratmanova, taking the first of two loads of our gear and giving us a chance to assess the ice. The ride brought three surprises. The first two came within a few miles of Uelen: First we saw a polar bear and two cubs along the coast, and later we got a great view of a killer whale frolicking in the surf. The third and most remarkable surprise unfolded all the way to Ratmanova: The Strait was virtually wide open. Only one chain of ice pans extending as a loose barrier along the island's coast loomed as an obstacle. And even that one looked as if it could be negotiated with minimal effort.

Andrei, who had accompanied us on this flight, was grinning ear to ear. I exchanged the "thumbs up" sign with him.

When we dropped our four team members off near the island's patrol station with our dogs and equipment, they fully expected to see us again that evening arriving by boat. But by the time our second load of equipment had been flown over, it was too late in the day to start a boat journey. We hoped that reports of continuing stable weather were accurate.

The night was a restless one. Nervous excitement kept me

up. The calm weather and ice-free water seemed auspicious signs. Well before six in the morning I was up and on the radio to Anne to announce our plans to launch the crossing.

By midmorning we had the baidar loaded on a sled, and with the help of snow machines and numerous townspeople were maneuvering down the coastline, looking for a suitable place to launch. The ice that had vacated the Strait now crowded the shores near Uelen, and we had to tow our baidar several miles before reaching an accessible channel.

The day was getting on. Worse yet, we'd lost our clear weather. Foreboding dark clouds hung in the western sky. An occasional blustery wind kicked up the shoreline snow. After a quick team huddle we accepted the fact that today's plans were washed out. We had three choices. We could return to Uelen and get some rest. We could set camp out here so we would be ready to depart first thing in the morning. Or we could use the afternoon to take a practice run in the boat and return to Uelen that evening.

For me there was no question. It was imperative that we use this time for training. I saw it as a gift. My Soviet friends weren't about to buy that line of logic. Most of them, tired and damp with perspiration from the long transport, were inclined to return to town. Sasha was most adamant, but I stood my ground, insisting on the training.

As the debate grew, so did my anger. No excuse could be made, I felt, for not taking full advantage of this opportunity to train. "Listen!" I finally shouted to Sasha, "I'm responsible for the lives of the American team members. The rest of you can do what you want, but I and the other Americans are going to give that boat a try."

Sasha exploded. Pointing a finger at my chest and yelling in Russian, he gave me a thorough tongue-lashing. I gathered that his point had not so much to do with the training as it did with my making a distinction about the Americans.

I respected his insistence that we were one team and not two. All of us had carefully tried to honor that ideal throughout the journey. Soviet-American teamwork was, after all, one prin-cipal goal of the project. But in this case, a distinct difference was at work. While Dmitry and I as co-leaders shared a moral responsibility for the lives of all the team members, only I bore a legal liability.

Having been involved in outdoor program leadership for years, I knew full well that if an accident occurred on this trek and an American court found me guilty of negligence, my family and I could face damages that could result in financial ruin. That concept was foreign to the Soviets and I couldn't articulate it to them out there, given our communication limits and a steadily worsening wind chill.

In the end Dmitry agreed to the training and soothed Sasha. We moved the boat to the water's edge and gently slid it in. It looked stable and seaworthy. We donned our knee-high boots, yellow spray suits and life jackets. Mounds of gear were piled on board in helter-skelter fashion. Team members groped their way through the mess to find a place to park themselves.

I don't know if any of us had really intended for this trial run to represent a worst-case scenario, but it certainly served as one. The boat, loaded nearly to the gunwales, was terribly top heavy and poorly balanced. Some team members jammed their legs between packs. Others sat cross-legged on top of them. A dog sled teetered precariously across the boat. A jumble of skis hung out over the side.

The scene was ridiculous, and, had we not been maneuvering in a small protected pocket of calm water, it would have been unacceptably dangerous. If this contraption went over in the open seas, our spray suits, boots and life vests would offer little help, but, I reasoned, the exercise would make it strikingly apparent to everyone that we had to get our act together before attempting this journey.

Lonnie had already opted out, choosing to stay on shore. Dmitry attempted to coax him on board. When Dmitry persisted, Lonnie stood firm—and shouted an angry curse.

It was the first time I'd heard Lonnie use profanity when talking to another team member. Something had snapped in his mind.

Something was about to snap in mine.

The ice had shifted and opened a channel between our little "training pool" and the open sea beyond. This channel gave some of our passengers a wild idea. Excited chatter rippled through the boat. I couldn't believe what I was hearing. Some of the team members were suggesting that we go for it.

Even without any obstacles, the 30-mile boat journey would take at least four hours. To be safe, we would need to allow twice as much time. It was now nearly three in the afternoon— only six hours of daylight remained—and we had not even begun rethinking and reorganizing our load.

The suggestion to set out for Ratmanova was soundly shot down, but I was shaken by the bravado and foolhardiness it reflected.

We pulled the boat up on shore. While the others worked on the load, Vadim and I searched on a snow machine for a better place to launch the boat the next day. Winds were clogging our coast with ice. We found a good launch site two miles away.

I looked off into the fog that hid Ratmanova. I wondered how we would ever find that five-mile long lump of rock with only compasses for navigation. Offshore winds were kicking up rollers several feet high.

My daughter Bria's face came sharply into focus in my mind. Was it worth it? Was it worth it to subject myself and my teammates to the dangers of these near-freezing ocean waters all for the sake of fulfilling an objective of this expedition?

To symbolically open the Bering Strait by crossing it in the manner the natives used for thousands of years was important to me. Given the overwhelming enthusiasm Chukotkans had expressed for our plans, I knew that it was important to them too. But how much risk should we take in the process? With our current state of organization, I decided, we faced too much risk.

When we returned to town that evening, I called a major team meeting. We gathered in a school office. I explained that I needed to hear from each team member on two questions: Did they feel our plan to cross the Strait in a baidar was safe? Did they feel the plan was important?

Andrei and Anatoly had joined us. I assured them that the meeting was not a hearing on their seamanship or the quality of their boat. I felt confident in their skills, but neither they nor their ancestors had traveled on the ocean at this time of year.

155

Only in summer did Eskimos make journeys across the open seas.

" I know the baidar is a good boat," I said to the group. "But if there's a problem, if water comes in the boat or people go in the water, our bodies will last only about 30 minutes in that cold sea. We're laying our lives on the line.

"As Ernie put it so well to me this afternoon," I continued, "it's a good boat for people who know what they're doing, who know the area they're traveling in and who have a damn good reason for traveling in that boat under dangerous conditions. Do we fit that profile?"

The discussion that ensued was long and convoluted. Sasha and Alexander took turns interpreting.

Dmitry was impatient with the meeting. He was always reluctant to spend time discussing issues when he felt that all that was needed was action. Why the need for discussion? he asked. Anybody who is uncomfortable with the plan can simply go across by helicopter.

It wasn't that simple for me. As co-leader I felt it would be flagrantly irresponsible to let any team members set off in that boat without both Dmitry and me on board, and I wasn't about to step in that boat unless the configuration was radically different than the setup of that afternoon.

Ginna acknowledged the fears.

"Like anyone who's grown up in Alaska and lived in rural coastal villages, I've lost many friends in accidents in the water." But she was willing to go for it if changes were made.

"I would like us to take two rubber rafts along for safety and I would like many kilograms removed from the load. We've got a few days to experiment and I trust the leadership."

Ernie, still reckoning with his son's death, drew his thoughts from his years of travel in coastal waters as a fisherman.

"The baidar is safe," he said, "but no matter how good you're prepared, you can't control the natural conditions. Just like that anything could happen.

"We could have high winds. The ice pack could puncture a hole in the boat. I'm willing to go in the boat, but we must realize that anything could happen."

Sasha and Vadim were willing to go in the boat. Lonnie

would go over by helicopter and join Robert, Darlene, Zoya and Cola.

We agreed on a plan. To lighten the load we would not carry camping gear. We simply would not set out unless the weather, the ice, the visibility and the timing all indicated that we could get to Ratmanova before nightfall. Two six-person rafts would be towed and we'd all carry safety flares. Alexander would stay in radio contact with the border patrol. Dmitry would make certain that the border patrol kept a helicopter on standby in Uelen during the first half of our journey and then moved it to Ratmanova for the second half. The patrol could, in theory, respond within 20 minutes to an SOS anywhere along our route.

This most intense and—for me at least—most meaningful team huddle of the expedition had lasted nearly two hours. Having a plan that would substantially enhance the safety of our undertaking left me much relieved. I drew an equal sense of satisfaction just from having gone through an exercise in which we connected as a team. It would still be a risky venture but now at least I knew the mind set of the people I'd be sharing these risks with.

Given our communication obstacles and delays for translations and clarifications, the meeting had taken a great deal of energy and effort. It left us all drained, but there was no question in my mind that it was worth it. Characteristically, there was doubt in Dmitry's mind. Looking pale and haggard, he leaned toward me as the meeting was breaking up and said, "We have taken much time and what have we gained? This meeting was not important."

I was appalled. What did he mean? How could he think that way? So many times he had discounted or discouraged the team discussions that I proposed. It left me absolutely perplexed and often angry.

Ironically, he steadfastly supported handling issues democratically. He was a fervent proponent of consensus rule on day-to-day decisions like our meal and mileage schedule. But he opposed discussion or debate. It seemed he loved referendums but hated campaigns.

What was the cultural gap, I wondered, that led to such diametrically different opinions between us on the value of meetings? I thought long and hard about it and discussed it often with other team members. My queries to Dmitry about it were answered with a shrug and the refrain, "Why need meetings? Why need meetings?"

I didn't learn the answer until after the expedition was over. The answer came as I read transcripts of an interview Dmitry did with the *National Geographic* film crew producing a documentary on the expedition.

In this interview, which was filmed after we ended our trek, Dmitry was asked if he and I argued. No, he answered through an interpreter, but he said, "Paul more than us strove toward some sort of general discussion, all of this called by one word—meeting. But in the Soviet Union," he continued, "the word for meeting carries somewhat ironic nuances, especially now during perestroika. Everyone a long time ago got fed up with meeting. Our perestroika means that the epoch of meetings, the epoch of meaningless discussions, is all in the past. You don't have to meet—you have to *do*. But here Paul somehow returned to our past and constantly tried to discuss everything."

Later in the interview Dmitry reflected on the issue again, saying that what he called my favorite word, "plans," had for him "a certain humorous sound. It sounds like Soviet reality," he said. "The last guys [Soviet leaders] made up lots of plans and had a lot of enthusiasm for their plans. But these plans are never fulfilled. So what's the sense of talking about these plans?"

When I read these transcripts of the interviews after the expedition, it all made sense to me. I could empathize with his distaste for meetings. I wished, though, that he had explained it to me earlier, when it mattered.

The evening of our baidar meeting, the last evening we were to spend on the Soviet mainland, also included another meeting for me—this time with Ginna. We both had items on the agenda. She felt slighted that I hadn't made her privy to all the information being transmitted and received during the many radio contacts I'd made with our Nome base the past few days. She was right. I had been negligent in taking time to keep her apprised of details. Now that we were about to enter the U.S., the organizational "baton" needed to be passed from the Soviet to the American team members. Given her Alaskan connections, Ginna's role with expedition logistics would take on increasing importance.

My agenda item was another issue that would be affected by our entry into Alaska—Ginna's relationship with Sasha. If the gossip mill was already at work in Chukotka, how much more active would it be when we hit the states? I wondered.

After a few moments of discussion, Ginna said that she would agree to my request that she and Sasha keep a low profile during the Alaskan segment of the trek. She added, though, "I'm a 30-year-old woman. I need to make my own decisions about how I handle my life."

In the end I decided to trust her handling of the matter. Ginna is one of the most competent people I have ever met, so surely, I thought, she would make sensible decisions on this matter. I resolved not to bring it up again. There was no point meddling in their affections any longer. That was only serving to stir up aggravation between us.

The night after the baidar meeting and my discussion with Ginna was a restless one for me. A kaleidoscope of concerns tumbled through my mind. I was up pacing the floors at 5:30 a.m. and then rousted Lonnie just so I could have somebody to talk to.

"I've got the heebie-jeebies bad," I told him, "If all the conditions aren't absolutely 100 percent today, I'm not going to go in that boat."

The weather looked tolerable. The sun shone through a gauze of cirrus clouds, and the northwest wind was light. Although the temperature on previous days had hovered around the freezing point, it had now dropped to about 15 degrees. As soon as I stepped outside I felt the chill and was glad to see signs of a stable high-pressure weather system.

The team shared a breakfast of porridge made on our campstoves in the gym's weight room. The mood was solemn. Our plans to launch would depend on what we saw on another reconnaissance flight. The border patrol agreed to take us up at nine. Ginna joined me and Dmitry and one of our guides for the flight while the other team members began moving gear out to the baidar, which was parked on the shelf ice five miles east of town.

What we saw from that flight looked like a miracle. A huge tongue of ice extended down into the Strait, but the leading edge of the ice formed a gentle arch from Cape Dezhnev, the tip of the continent, to Ratmanova. All we needed to do was follow the edge of the ice. In addition to guiding our way, the mantle of pack ice ensured calm water to the south and a refuge from the water if troubles arose. To be sure, there were a few obstacles. The tongue was shattered in places, leaving mile-wide gaps of open water with rolling waves and an occasional maze of ice shards and blind channels. Otherwise, though, conditions were as good as could be hoped for.

We were ecstatic as we returned to Uelen. The helicopter dropped us off at our baidar. Ginna and I set off on foot to find a route over which we could slide the baidar on its sled to the nearest open channel, nearly two miles away. The best route we could find was a rough one that threaded its way up and down hummocks of ice as tall as we. I knew we could muscle the 500 pound boat through there with help from snow machines, but it was already noon. Could we do it fast enough?

Moments later the team members arrived and tackled the job with gusto.

With the boat teetering on a six-foot sled, a snow machine tugged in front and the team pushed from behind. We gained a few feet at a time with each thrust. For awhile it looked doubtful that the job could be done in time. Furthermore, ice from the north was steadily pinching off our channel. We were in a race against the clock.

By one o'clock we hadn't yet reached the halfway point. We redoubled our efforts and, after establishing a routine of push and pull, began sliding the boat along faster and faster. We reached the water's edge a little before two. But we still had to prepare the rafts and organize the load and the radio equipment. We were cutting into the precious six hours of daylight that we all agreed allowed an adequate margin for making the journey. At five minutes to three we hopped on board and cast off. After a few agonizing sputters the motor roared to life, and we began gliding down the channel. *"Che sleevah, che sleevah!"*(good luck!), hollered the hunters from Uelen who had helped us move the boat.

And then we were alone with the ice and the sea and the soft putter of the motor.

I looked to Ernie for reassurance. "The boat is riding real well," he said.

Ginna asked if I wanted to say a prayer with her. I took her hand and we prayed for a safe ride. We also prayed for help in finding the island. At this point Ratmanova was hidden by fog, but with the ice edge to follow we figured we could find it with little difficulty.

The boat plowed through the water at about 10 miles an hour. Andrei wielded a massive wooden tiller in the rear, calling out instructions to Anatoly, who controlled the motor, to speed up or slow down depending on the waves and the brash ice. An occasional thud rippled through the boat as we hit a submerged block of ice. Anatoly quickly cut the motor to avoid damage to the propeller. Vadim sat up high in the bow on the lookout for such blocks, but they were hard to see.

Alexander, our Soviet radio operator, worked unsuccessfully at making contact with the base in Uelen. Though I was starting to relax a bit, the worry on his face didn't make it any easier for me to relax my death grip on the boat rail. Dmitry and Sasha sat behind us, studying their charts and compass.

The 100-yard-wide channel we followed swung south and then tapered to a near close. Beyond were the sweeping cliffs of Cape Dezhnev and a huge expanse of open water. We squeezed our way out of the channel. Had we arrived here a short time later, there wouldn't have been an easy exit.

We swung hard to the east, embarking on our journey along the tongue of ice. I could see more ice miles to the south, but for now we had clear sailing.

Like flight attendants, Ginna and Sasha began passing out snacks, lots of them—cheese, crackers, raisins, sausage, chocolate and coffee. I wasn't hungry, but the food served to ease the tension. I was able to soak in the fabulous scene around me and somewhat enjoy the experience.

Thousands of seabirds darkened sections of the southern

sky. Filtering through sea smoke and low-lying clouds, sunlight cast a shimmery bronze tint to the ocean surface, giving it the sheen of liquid metal. To the left we watched a large dark animal clamber onto a distant ice flow. "Sea lion," said Vadim.

We plowed through more brash ice—textured slush that came in a variety of shapes. Some was like floating gravel, other like candlesticks bunched together and upright. My favorite was the "polar bear track"—circlets of ice about the size and shape of polar bear paws.

A light snow squall passed over us, hiding the cliffs of the Soviet mainland. We moved along in the same whirl of white we'd so often found ourselves in on the tundra. I found it far more disconcerting to be in a whiteout on the sea than on land. I was obliged to sit passively, trusting that Andrei and Anatoly would pilot the craft to safety. I consoled myself that it was nearly as natural for them to be plying these waters in a walrus skin boat as it was for the seals we could see bobbing in and out of the surf. But Andrei had never negotiated this stretch of water before.

I was completely out of my element. I considered how relative courage and comfort are. Being tagged an "adventurer" doesn't exempt one from fear.

Halfway across, the ice edge was abruptly interrupted by huge gaps of open water that extended as far north as we could see. We held our compass bearing as we crossed the gap, expecting to meet the ice again. A light north wind stirred up erratic rollers. At times the waters crested higher than our heads, raising another wave of queasiness in my gut.

"How does it feel trusting your destiny to an eighth of an inch of walrus hide and a couple of inches of freeboard?" I hollered to Ginna. She shook her head and continued to clutch the seat. Ernie looked up and nodded benignly, his way of letting me know that everything was still OK.

The baidar performed exquisitely. Andrei would swing tight on the tiller to catch each wave on the diagonal. The hull shuddered as it hit the wave and then slid harmlessly down the trough. We'd look out at a wall of water and then begin to rise again. An occasional spray lapped overboard. We also had a slight leak around the motor mount, and several inches of water sloshed under the planks on the floor, not enough, though, to cause any concern.

I was struck by how well-suited the baidar was for these conditions. Clearly its design elements—the height of the prow, the graceful arch of hull and the taper at bow and stern—all had evolved over thousands of years of trial and error by Eskimo hunters to match the demands of the Bering Sea. The baidar was tailored to tackle the size and shape of the waves we were encountering.

An hour later we reentered calmer waters along the floe edge, but large pans blocked direct passage to the east. We veered southward, searching for a way through. Fog still hid Ratmanova.

Sasha was studying his compass intently.

"Do you know where we're going?" I asked. Sasha just looked up at me and smiled.

Now that we were within 20 miles of the island, an errant bearing could cause us to miss it.

We ran up against blocks wedged tightly together. Anatoly shut the engine down while Vadim pried the blocks apart with the oars. Our progress was slow.

In the distance we could hear the pulse of a helicopter. We listened for several minutes. From the ever-changing sound, it was apparent that it was searching for us in a grid pattern. It drew closer. Suddenly we could see it hovering a hundred feet above the water a quarter-mile south of us.

"We're here! We're here!" we yelled and waved. With our bright yellow spray suits and orange life rafts in tow, I felt certain we'd be easy to spot. We weren't though. The helicopter disappeared in the clouds.

Alexander tried anxiously to reach the helicopter by radio but couldn't make contact. Our contingency plan for rescue by helicopter was obviously far from fool-proof. Despite the generous efforts of the border patrol to track us, our survival was in our own hands.

Making contact with the helicopter would not just offer some reassurance. It also would confirm our bearing. I would welcome such assurance.

It was obvious that Vadim didn't share my concern. The

seals we had seen triggered his hunting instincts. He perched in the prow with our gun in hand. When a walrus surfaced he went for a kill. The deafening report of gunfire caught half the team members by surprise. "My God, did the engine blow up?" asked Ginna, looking up with a start.

Fortunately the shot went wide. "How did you think we would haul that carcass to Ratmanova?" I asked Vadim. Though he had missed the shot, Vadim looked absolutely blissful. He was truly in his element out here.

We heard the helicopter again. This time it burst through the clouds almost directly overhead. The pilot swooped down. Photographers hung out of the bay doors and open windows to get what was certain to be some spectacular footage. We wove our way through sculpted blocks of ice, some of which rose well over our heads.

The pilot cut a tight circle less than 50 feet above the surface just behind us. A blast of prop wash stirred up a heavy spray and overturned our life rafts. Our two jerry cans of extra fuel went bobbing off into the waves. It was time to stop the media circus. The pilots motioned their apologies. We held up our charts by way of asking direction. They pointed a bit left of our current bearing and then disappeared into the clouds. After retrieving our fuel cans, we carried on with confidence.

A little before seven o'clock, Alexander shouted. Land!

Through a break in the clouds we could see the cliff tops of Ratmanova about a mile away, dappled in light from a sun that had already dipped below the horizon. Had the clouds and fog been more persistent we might have missed the island altogether. Our course had been taking us to the south.

Andrei swung left and we surveyed the coastline for a place to land. Pans and rubble blocked our access to the north end, where the patrol station was, so we had to settle on a spot about halfway up the five-mile-long western shore. Even there several hundred yards of mush separated us from the shelf ice. We wedged our way through. Some of us pried blocks apart with poles. Others jumped on the partially frozen mush to loosen it while keeping hands on the gunwales for safety. Anatoly would ram the boat forward with a thrust from the motor, bringing its bow up the ice to force it down like an icebreaker.

VADIM
Hunter at sea

As we neared shore, the mush made progress even more difficult. Andrei brought out a long rope. We laid the oars on the soft ice to bridge the gaps between ice chunks. We climbed out of the baidar, walked on the oars across the gaps and then heaved on the line to tug the baidar forward inch by inch. It was after nine o'clock and nearly dark when we had the baidar safely on firm shelf ice.

Giddy with joy, I let out a couple of good hollers. The others handled our arrival more stoically. Only Ginna shared my exuberance. I gave her a big kiss on the cheek.

Alexander hadn't been able to make radio contact with anyone on the island, so we had to find the patrol station on our own.

After putting on dry clothes and finishing our food, we were on our way again. The patrol station was two miles away.

Our first half-mile of shelf ice was a quagmire of deep pits filled with powdery snow and slush. It took us nearly an hour to slog our way through and reach the towering rock pinnacle and ramparts of ice that marked that shore. Around the north corner, the shoreline dropped off steeply into a soup of ice blocks and slush-filled water. We groped our way through the dark, sometimes on all fours, along the base of the cliff.

It was nearing midnight. At one point we had to notch footholds into the steep wall of ice and snow to make our way. The sea glistened below in the hazy glow of moonlight.

As we rounded a corner, a magnificent sight greeted us. There on a clifftop a half-mile ahead was the border patrol station. It was bathed in light. The officers, uncertain of our whereabouts, had done everything possible to guide us. All the lights in the complex were on. Searchlights swept the shore. A lighthouse beamed out to sea. At the base of the cliffs a huge bonfire was blazing, and on the rooftops the soldiers were setting off green flares.

We let out a wild whoop and flashed our headlamps toward the station. Everyone there responded with a roar of cheers. Rising above all their words of welcome were cries of joy from Zoya. "Oy! Oy! Oy!" she screamed. She scrambled down the hill and raced up the shore to greet us. Lonnie, Robert, Darlene and Cola followed her. What a joyous reunion! We smothered each other in hugs.

We also shared with our greeting party a special telegram we had received before departing Uelen. It meant the world to me. Addressed to "the members of the Bering Bridge Expedition," it was from General Secretary Mikhail Gorbachev:

> *I am greeting you with all my heart, you the members of the Soviet-American expedition with the name* The Bering Bridge. *The name is not just a symbol for me. This name represents my own true feelings. You are truly helping to build a bridge of friendship and cooperation between Chukotka and Alaska as well as between the Soviet Union and the United States. We are united by common challenges such as preserving northern culture, protecting the arctic ecosystem and, of course, the most important challenge, the strengthening of peaceful relations among all countries of the world. I wish you the best of luck, great success and may all your goals be accomplished.*

The team and helpers tugged and pushed the baidar toward the sea.

With no time to spare they pushed off into the icy waters.

An eighth of an inch of walrus skin between sea and crew.

NINE

ДЕВЯТЬ

From our reunion on the shelf ice, we climbed a nearly vertical slope to the patrol station on a ledge.

The base commander, a handsome man with a manicured mustache and high, black leather boots, greeted us with a warm handshake and led us toward the main building. It was surprisingly quaint—a two-story gray stucco structure with red trim, tall deep-set windows and a pitched roof. It reminded me of a little hotel I once stayed at in West Germany's Black Forest.

I stopped to read the etched-glass sign alongside the main building's massive wooden door. "Soviet Border Patrol," it said, and at the bottom—"A Division of the KGB." For the first time we were aware of that connection.

Soldiers in fatigues greeted us in the lobby. I was struck by how young they were. Many looked to be in their teens.

They led us into a tiny dining hall. Lacy curtains, cheery woodland murals and white shutters over the serving window made me think of that Black Forest hotel again. As we took our seats, I mentioned that to Robert. He gave one of his robust laughs and said, "No, Paul, you've just been out on the ice too long."

The meal was simple but delicious—dark bread, tea and that ravioli-type dish we had been introduced to back in our first village.

The long day's tension had drained us thoroughly. With

warm food in our bellies, we could hardly keep our eyes open. We went to a small house nearby, where cots and sleeping bags had been crammed in tiny rooms for us.

I arose early in the morning, eager to explore our surroundings here in the most remote reach of the Soviet world. Three sides of the central courtyard were framed by the main building, a utilities complex and a warehouse. The fourth side of the courtyard was formed by exercise equipment built of pipe, cable and tires. Its worn condition indicated heavy use by the soldiers.

A series of narrow walkways that had been carved through chest-high drifts of snow connected the court with our barracks and the officers' quarters, a new two-story house. Its occupants included the commander, his wife—who was the island's only woman—and their six-year-old daughter.

Soldiers with shovels made from plywood and broomsticks scraped fresh drifts from the walkways, loaded the snow on a metal skid and dumped it down a cliff face. I joined them and looked over the edge. The site served as a dumping ground for all of the station's trash, which was washed by rain and melting snow into the sea.

The outhouse—a six-holer—also overhung the ravine. The stench from it was almost overwhelming, but inside I found one feature I hadn't seen in any other outhouses in Chukotka—toilet paper. It was coarse and heavy, like gas-station paper for cleaning windshields, but it was a vast improvement over the shreds of newspaper and cardboard that were available in other outhouses we'd visited.

I walked along the edge of the ravine a ways to see if I could catch a view of Little Diomede. Before I had gone more than a few yards, I heard some commotion from the sentry post. Looking up I saw a rifle-toting soldier leaning out an open window and staring blankly at me. I remembered Dmitry's comment at breakfast: Our one rule here was never to step beyond designated pathways without an escort.

With two days to go before embarking by dog sled for the Date Line ceremony, our task on Ratmanova was to make plans for reaching mainland Alaska. We intended to continue from

Little Diomede by baidar after the event. Twenty-two miles of Bering Strait still separated us from Wales, our first village in Alaska. Winds had backed the ice up tight against the northern side of the islands. Perhaps open channels still existed to the south. To find out, the helicopter pilots took us up.

From the air we saw that to the west—toward Chukotka—the Strait was choked again with huge pans of ice. Yesterday's passageway had been a stroke of great fortune. We also saw that a narrow channel existed between the spot where our baidar was parked on the ice shelf and the south end of the island. Although we couldn't see eastward beyond Little Diomede, it seemed that the pans to the south were far enough apart that we could snake our way through them toward Wales. Of course, these conditions could change rapidly.

It was essential that we position our baidar for the crossing on the leeward side of the island—the south—before more channels were closed. Moving the boat would be a daylong project, so we made plans to send a crew over to move it the first thing in the morning.

The courtyard came alive in the afternoon when the soldiers came out for their Saturday soccer match. We watched from the sidelines for awhile, then they challenged us to a game. A bystander kept score in the snow for "KGB vs. BBE" (Bering Bridge Expedition).

The soldiers were outstanding players. Tromping about on glare ice in heavy parkas and knee-high fur and leather boots, they dazzled us with moves that would impress the pros. Most of our team members were neophytes. Fortunately Vadim, Cola and Robert knew a few tricks and managed to keep us from getting slaughtered.

No one thought much about the score, though. All of us, soldiers and adventurers, were reveling in the joy of having fun together in such an unlikely setting. I knew the barriers had fully broken down when we started cross-checking each other with abandon and laughing about it.

The soldiers invited us to present our community program after the scheduled Saturday-night entertainment, a war film. I watched a portion of it from the doorway of the meeting hall. The movie featured one scene after another of Soviet World War

II fighters on combat missions. As enemy planes burst into balls of fire, the soldiers responded with loud applause.

Minutes later we were on stage talking to them about goodwill and friendship, and their applause was equally enthusiastic. I guess these were men for all seasons.

They were particularly curious about Little Diomede, and pressed Robert with many questions about village life. The scout post they staff on Ratmanova's east cape overlooks the settlement on Little Diomede. The soldiers said they were grateful to have been entertained during the past year, watching the town's new water tank being welded together.

Something else they saw through binoculars left them distraught. Often they had seen pans of ice pass through the Strait carrying the headless carcasses of walrus. It was obvious that the animals had been slaughtered for their ivory tusks. How could the U.S. allow such carnage? they asked. Robert said he shared their concern. He explained that poachers from mainland Alaska were responsible. The people of his village, he said, kill only animals they intend to fully consume.

The patrol commander and a younger officer played guitar and sang for us. They presented each of us with a gift, a section of caribou antler on which they had etched greetings to our team and a scene of their station.

Then they brought a green wooden obelisk into the room. It was about six feet tall and mounted on a wide pedestal. This monument, the commander announced, would be placed on the ice at the Date Line during our crossing ceremony and later would be displayed in a Soviet museum. Handing over a paint brush and can of white paint, he invited us to place our signatures on the pedestal. We finished the evening with a visit to their banya.

In the morning I just couldn't get out of bed. I expected it. In the banya the night before, my system crashed. Lying on the cedar bench nearest the wood stove, I had felt my body finally release the stresses and strains of our crossing.

After breakfast, the boat crew set off for the baidar without me while Lonnie and Cola headed by dog sled around the west side of the island to break a trail for our trip to the Date Line the next morning.

I didn't see any of them again until nightfall. I spent most of the day in bed, getting up occasionally to attempt radio contact with Anne Walker at our base. Static from the patrol station's equipment blocked my transmissions to Nome, but I was able to reach Little Diomede. Instructions were relayed to us from there to arrive at the Date Line at 11:30 a.m. Alaska time.

During the afternoon of my recovery day, the commander's young daughter sought me out to help her dig tunnels in the snowbanks.

"Where are these going?" I asked her in Russian.

"Ah, America," she answered with a smile.

Our baidar crew returned at dusk with bad news. They'd had great difficulty getting back to the boat. By the time they reached it, was too late in the day to attempt a launching. We would just have to hope that these calm, clear weather conditions held.

Lonnie and Cola returned from their mission with the news that a good trail was in place toward the Date Line, but that they had encountered bitter winds between the islands. That was an ominous sign. The steep walls of Little and Big Diomede create a venturi effect, constricting and accelerating air flow through the region. High winds in the channel suggest nasty weather is moving into the area.

A radio call to Little Diomede confirmed our suspicions. Weather over the Alaskan side of the Strait was forecast to deteriorate throughout the day. Fog trapped 80 journalists, supporters and state officials, including the governor, in Nome, some 100 miles away. The National Guard Blackhawk helicopters waiting to carry them to the Date Line would be grounded at least another hour and possibly all day. Once again, weather plagued what we hoped would be a high-profile event.

Nonetheless, the plans were still set for the ceremony. The Soviet helicopters were expected to arrive on time. Some of the American contingent, including National Guardsmen and a few journalists, already had arrived at Little Diomede.

Waving goodbye to our hosts, we embarked at nine for our short journey to the Date Line. The weather on our side of the island was calm and mostly sunny, but as soon as we rounded the corner heading toward Little Diomede we felt the blast of a stiff north ground wind. We could see the tops of both islands just fine, but the satellite dish that marked the location for the ceremony was hidden. Fortunately, some of the Soviet patrol had gone on ahead, providing snow machine tracks that we could follow as we headed toward the center of the two-and-a-half-mile channel that separates the islands.

We plunged blindly along and were just a hundred feet away before we could see the ceremony site. Some 30 or so people were milling about near the satellite dish, a portable telecast station and a small receiving platform. Soviet and American flags mounted on tall steel standards were snapping loudly in the wind. As we drew closer we could see an orange line that had been spray painted on the ice to mark the Soviet-American border. National Guardsmen and Soviet border patrol soldiers stood at attention on their respective sides of the line.

We were instructed to pass between them. They congratulated us and their counterparts across the line as we skied by them and on toward a platform that had been set up for the occasion. There, arm in arm, we posed for photos.

The weather severely curtailed the event. The Alaskan governor's delegation had remained in Nome, socked in by fog. Journalists who were part of the weather-bound group had to cover the event by telephone.

The Chukotkan governor's delegation had arrived in Little Diomede, but because of the severe ground winds only one of the four Soviet helicopters proceeded to the International Date Line. When it landed near us we obliged a request to reenact our crossing of the line for the 20 Soviet journalists on board. By this time we were all so thoroughly chilled and windburned that no one minded adjourning this makeshift ceremony and moving on to Little Diomede.

We were a proud and happy crew, but none of us was overwhelmed with emotion. After all, having worked together for nearly two months, we had already crossed the line that separates Soviets and Americans. Though we had looked forward to the Date Line ceremony, the border no longer held any

ROBERT
Million-dollar smile

great significance for us. We knew full well now that it was just an arbitrary line that separates governments but not the hearts of the people. The International Date Line had become just one more point on our route.

Our excitement was focused mainly on the places that lay ahead. Our Soviet friends were eager to see Alaska for the first time. And Robert could hardly contain his enthusiasm about going home to Little Diomede.

There in the comfort of the village's dazzling school complex, the real celebration took place. The Diomeders, our team members and a few dozen other Americans joined some 80 Soviets, including Governor Kobetz, Chukotkan officials and many Soviet Eskimos for a four-hour festival. The village dance company opened with an hour of music and dance. Robert jumped in and performed with more gusto than I'd ever seen. Then followed a series of speeches.

Governor Kobetz explained that although Governor Cowper could not attend, the two of them had signed the protocol to loosen travel restrictions between Alaska and Chukotka.

There was a genuine spirit of fellowship among participants. But for many members of our team this event, like the Date Line ceremony, seemed so canned and rushed and confused that it was hard to sink our hearts into it. That was just as well because we needed all the concentration we had for the strange episode that was about to unfold.

At 4:00 p.m., with the weather worsening, the Soviet delegation boarded the four Aeroflot helicopters to return to Lavrentiya. Word went out that two members of their delegation were unaccounted for. A passenger list showed 84 people, but pilots reported that only 82 had returned. A quick search was made, but when nothing turned up the discrepancy was dismissed as a miscount and the helicopters took off.

At least that's the way the situation was presented to me. It struck me as odd that there could be a miscount.

Dmitry and Alexander were talking by radio to their Soviet expedition base in Lavrentiya when they received confirmation by radio that two Soviets were missing. It was nearly midnight when they got the news. Dmitry called me and Ginna into the room. His face was sunken. He looked more gaunt and weary than I'd ever seen him.

When I asked Dmitry if he thought a defection had taken place, he looked at the floor and nodded. My heart went out to him. He obviously felt obligated to shoulder a lot of responsibility for the incident. It was his expedition office in Moscow that had handled most of the Soviet arrangements for this event.

Ginna pointed out that the missing people might not necessarily have defected. Perhaps they wandered out toward the Date Line and got lost in the storm. That was possible. Even our team members had had trouble following the snow machine tracks through the whiteout to find the village. But if the two Soviets were lost, there was no way they could survive the night out there. Without shelter and proper clothing, they'd hardly last an hour in this storm.

Perhaps we should begin a search of the town, we thought. If we take any action at all, I cautioned, we must alert the National Guard commander, Colonel Wurtmann. He was the ranking authority on the island and we would be stepping beyond our bounds to do anything without his knowledge. Ginna and I headed up to the village's National Guard armory, a corrugated metal structure in the middle of town. A sleepy-eyed Guardsman answered the door and led us in past a dozen cots with snoring Guardsmen to Colonel Wurtman's bed.

"I'm sorry to awake you, sir," I said as he sat up in the dimly lit room. "but I'm afraid we have some difficult news. We've learned that two defectors may be present on the island."

He listened intently to our report but didn't respond. Then we told him of our plan to search the public buildings during the night and explained that if nothing turned up Robert would arrange a search of the homes in the morning. The colonel nodded and agreed to accompany us to the school to discuss the matter with our Soviet friends.

The colonel was curiously withdrawn but said that he and his men were ready to do whatever was deemed best. It was 2:30 a.m. and we were all exhausted. We decided to get some sleep and commence the search in the morning. We would begin at 6:00 a.m. to avoid disrupting the town.

On the way back to my barracks, standing alone on a hill, I scanned the village for places that might be appealing as hideouts. Piercing the darkness out toward the middle of the Strait was an unearthly glow coming up from the ice through the drifting snow. It gave me a start, but then I realized it was a safety light that had been left shining on the satellite dish. I made a mental note to make sure in the morning that our missing persons weren't seeking refuge in the portable telecast booth below the dish.

Then I noticed a large wooden hut near the shoreline where the Aeroflot helicopters had parked. That would make a convenient hideout, I thought. I groped my way down to the hut and found an opening on one end of the hut. I cautiously stepped inside.

When my eyes adjusted to the dim light filtering through an opening in the roof, I could see that snowplow equipment used for clearing the airstrip was stored here. The enclosed cab of that tractor would make a good hideout, I thought to myself.

I announced myself in Russian and English and stood waiting in the dark for a response. I felt foolish. My search seemed ridiculous. If the defectors were hiding here, they were probably scared out of their wits and would be unlikely to turn themselves over to someone who suddenly shows up in the darkness. It was far better, I thought to myself, to wait until morning light to pursue this. I walked back to the gym and collapsed in my sleeping bag on the floor.

Ginna woke me at six. "The colonel has something to tell you," she said. He was standing nearby.

"Did you find them?" I asked.

"No," he answered, "they turned themselves over to us."

"Oh, thank God," I said. "When? Early this morning?"

"No," he answered, "yesterday during the celebration."

I rubbed my eyes. He had known all along where the defectors were.

The missing people were young journalism students from Moscow. Shortly after their arrival in the Aeroflot helicopters, they quietly approached a National Guardsman and announced their intentions to apply for political asylum in the U.S. To avoid causing a scene during our Soviet-American celebration, the Guardsmen had hid the defectors in a room in the village clinic.

Governor Cowper and other high-ranking officials, including General John Schaeffer, who directs Alaska's National Guard, and Gary Johnson, regional director of the U.S. Immigration and Naturalization Service, had been alerted immediately. They too had agreed to hold the news. The first public announcement of the event was to be made that afternoon through a terse news release.

The reasons for the previous night's pretense were never explained to us. It didn't matter at this point. What mattered most dearly to us now that the defections had been confirmed was whether the incident would spoil the improved relations between Alaska and Chukotka and threaten the new trade and travel agreement.

The defections struck my teammates and me as inexcusably selfish. In one swoop these two individuals might have ruined everything that we and many Alaskans and Chukotkans were working toward.

I felt ripped off. They had used us. They had taken advantage of our goodwill event for their own gain.

I thought of all the proposals the Chukotkans had discussed with us about the school exchanges, trade initiatives and cultural festivals they hoped to have with their Alaskan neighbors. Would these be refused?

Perhaps the defectors weren't aware of the potential ramifications of their actions. Maybe they'd had second thoughts. Perhaps they were just waiting for an offer to return home.

The colonel agreed to let us speak with them.

They were staying in the armory and were lying awake on cots when we arrived. They sat up and greeted us cordially.

One spoke impeccable English and introduced himself as Anatoly Tkachenko. He was in his early 20s, had neatly combed brown hair and a clean shaven face and was wearing wool dress slacks and a blue and white striped sports top. His friend, Alexander Genkin, was about the same age and had light curly hair and strong Germanic features. Alexander spoke only Russian. Anatoly answered our questions.

I asked him if they were aware of the efforts under way in this region to improve Soviet-American relations. Yes, he said, they knew all about those efforts and our expedition.

Then why, I asked, had they chosen such a horribly inappropriate time to defect? Without pause he launched into a treatise about Soviet repressions at home and abroad. Their defection, he said, was an act of protest against their government.

It was a well-rehearsed rap. It was clear that they were committed to their actions and that no amount of discussion would change their minds. "We are sorry if we have caused any difficulties for your expedition," Alexander said. "But we felt this was our only chance."

I agreed with Anatoly's denouncement of repressive Soviet policies. I also empathized with their desire to defect. It wasn't the act that angered me; it was the timing. I fumed, but the irony of the situation didn't escape me. Here we were—stuck with these guys in a storm at a place that Jacques Cousteau once claimed to be one of the most inaccessible villages in the world.

Later, Dmitry also talked with the defectors. He demanded to know why they had done it. Anatoly told him they would have left legally if they could have. In a news story that came out much later, Anatoly said that he felt he had convinced Dmitry of his sincerity.

However, there was an odd twist to Anatoly's assessment. In talking with Dmitry later that morning, I sensed that the only thing Anatoly had convinced Dmitry of was that he and Alexander were not being held by the Guardsmen against their will.

It became apparent to me that some of our Soviet team members had wondered—for awhile at least—if this was a setup. It had occurred to them that perhaps the Guardsmen had talked or bribed Anatoly and Alexander into defecting as a way of making a public relations splash for democracy at a media event. Our Soviet friends now knew, of course, that nothing of the sort had taken place, but such was the confusion that engulfed our team that morning.

A weather report Monday evening indicated that the earliest the storm might break would be Wednesday morning. The National Guard announced plans to send helicopters out to pick up the defectors at the first opportunity. We were stuck together on the island for at least one more day.

In the meantime, we continued to make plans to cross the remaining 22 miles of Strait to reach the Alaskan mainland. I feared the storm was scuttling that plan by compacting the Strait with ice. The winds had probably already rendered our baidar inaccessible. We wouldn't know exactly what lay ahead until the storm broke and reconnaissance reports were received from the Soviet border patrol and Alaskan pilots.

Tuesday brought only added worries. We received word that some news services in the Lower 48 were reporting that the defectors were two of our team members. What next? I thought. I frantically called several reporters in Minnesota to ask that they clear up the errors in the stories.

In Nome, Anne Walker, our base manager, was stuck on the phone refuting rumors. One was particularly irksome. The scuttlebutt in Nome was that negotiations regarding native contacts between Alaska and Chukotka were being called off in response to the defections. Some people, she learned, were intimating that the Bering Bridge Expedition should be held responsible for this because of our association with the event.

The allegation hit her hard. Anne, who is half Inupiaq Eskimo, has a deep commitment to improved border relations and has been involved with the process in many ways.

As we hoped, the winds began lessening that evening. It appeared we would have a shot at leaving in the morning. Our team scrambled.

Dogs, sleds and much of our equipment were again to be taken over by aircraft. Jim Rowe, the owner of Bering Air in Nome and a staunch supporter of our project, offered to provide that service as part of his sponsorship. Cola, Lonnie, Darlene and Robert would accompany the dogs by airlift. Zoya would be the one new additional member of our boat crew. She had been reluctant to join us on the first leg of the crossing but, given the success of that one, was keen on being part of the second.

On our last evening in town we set our worries aside and enjoyed some fellowship with the villagers. Film that I had sent out to the States from Provideniya had been processed as slides. As planned, they were waiting for me on Little Diomede when we arrived. Over dinner that evening I poured over the hundreds of images and selected 80 to show. The show was as much of a treat for our team as it was for the hundred villagers who turned out to see it.

There we were on the screen—enjoying Eskimo dances with Chukotkans, shooing caribou away from our sleds, being embraced by village leaders as we entered their settlements, building snow-block walls to brace our tents against the storms and sharing tales of America with Chukchi school children.

Watching the show was a balm for me. All the tensions of the past few days drifted away, and I regained a strong sense of excitement and enthusiasm for our efforts to build the bridge. The feelings were reinforced by a roar of applause from the audience at the show's end.

According to plan, Dmitry and I awoke the team at 4:00 a.m. Sharing an oatmeal breakfast around a table in the gym, our team discussed the schedule.

The boat crew would head out immediately on a five-mile journey by ski back across the Date Line, past the patrol station and on around the west side of Ratmanova to our baidar. Cola would follow with one dog team, drop off our food and supplies at the boat and then return to Little Diomede before the airplane arrived. Robert, Lonnie and Darlene would move the remaining dogs, equipment and supplies to the airstrip on the sea ice in front of town and be on standby to load Jim's plane as soon as he arrived. With temperatures hovering around zero he would not be able to shut his engines down long on the runway without risking startup problems.

Our crew to pick up the boat set out across the channel at 6:30. The flights from Nome, including Jim's plane and the National Guard helicopters that would pick up the defectors, were to commence at 10:30. We carried a radio so Jim could let us know as soon as he crossed the Strait whether it was navigable. We expected to hear from him at eleven o'clock, about the same time that we would be in position to launch the boat.

We all were amazed to be able to casually ski back across the U.S.-Soviet border. No one was there to ask for passports and visas. The flags and obelisk had been removed from the middle of the channel. The orange line and snow machine tracks had been obliterated by the wind storm. Only the satellite dish remained.

"This is the way it's going to be for everybody someday!" I shouted over to Ginna, "They'll be able to just zip right on over to enjoy an afternoon soccer game with the boys in Ratmanova."

As we reached the shores of their island, six of the "boys" arrived by snow machine to greet us.

Anxious about ice conditions on the west side, we asked if their scouts had any reports. Yes, they said, and it didn't look good. From their vantage point on the clifftops the scouts observed that the channel we were counting on for reaching the south end of the island had a covering of ice. It could just be slush, they said. It was hard to tell from their position. Maybe we could push our way through, but we knew that would be a hellish task.

We hurried ahead with our fingers crossed. I think at this point we were all just hoping for a definitive answer—either "no problem" or "no go." We didn't want to take a chance on questionable conditions and perhaps get ourselves caught in a real mess.

By 9:30 we were on our way down the west shoreline. Pack ice near shore blocked our view of the Strait. I raced ahead and climbed a pinnacle of rock. From there, I accepted our moment of truth. It was definitive, all right. The baidar sat forlornly locked in ice that extended out at least a half mile. Beyond that the Strait was a patchwork of open channels and pans. It would be impossible to negotiate our way out of there by water.

I ran back and broke the news to the crew. In a way I felt more relieved than disappointed. Our safe arrival by baidar in Ratmanova had been the happy result of a great deal of good fortune, and I didn't want to push our luck. Most of the team seemed openly relieved by the news. They immediately set about making contingency plans.

Cola would continue on with his dog sled to retrieve the motor and other valuable supplies from the boat in case it should be washed out to sea. Dmitry would speak with the border patrol about securing the boat on dry ground. I took our portable radio and hurried back toward Little Diomede with hopes of contacting our pilot, Jim Rowe, to let him know that we would all need a lift on his flights.

As I crossed over the Soviet-American border for the third time, the Alascom crew was busy disassembling the satellite dish.

"The party's over!" one of them yelled to me as I skied past.

"Not for us!" I shouted back, "we've still got plenty of places to go and people to meet on this trek."

As I neared Diomede, it looked like an airshow was under way. Three helicopters and two airplanes were taking off or landing. Jim was among them with his Beech. I reached him on the radio and told him that our baidar was marooned.

"That's just as well," he answered. "The Alaskan side of the Strait is more ice than water. It would be impassable by either sled or boat." He said he'd be happy to take the entire expedition to Wales.

From a half mile out I watched a Blackhawk helicopter idling near the beach. Climbing on board were Guardsmen in uniform and two other men in plainclothes. The black fur hat one was wearing gave them away. Alexander and Anatoly were heading for Nome. Leaning on my ski poles, I watched them lift off. I was no longer angry with them. The incident was behind us.

The indications were that the defections had done no lasting harm. Ginna and I were told by a U.S. State Department official that the international negotiations would continue without interruption. Dmitry learned later that Soviet diplomats had resolved more or less to dismiss the incident as a cost of doing business.

Perhaps the greatest significance of the incident at the Date Line was that it made headlines worldwide. News of the defections drew the attention of people everywhere to our unique expedition. As a result the world was reawakened to the cultural bond between Soviet and American Eskimos.

A footnote: After Dmitry returned to Moscow, he reported to me that the press and government officials who discussed the expedition results with him made only passing reference to the defections. Dmitry detected no significant repercussions.

I also learned that when he had interviewed the defectors at the National Guard barracks in Little Diomede they made a request that left him incredulous:

Since they would not be using the return portion of their Aeroflot ticket from Moscow to Chukotka, they asked, would Dmitry be able to arrange for them to get a refund?

The KGB Border Patrol sign points the long way to Moscow.

Dmitry confronted the defectors on Little Diomede.

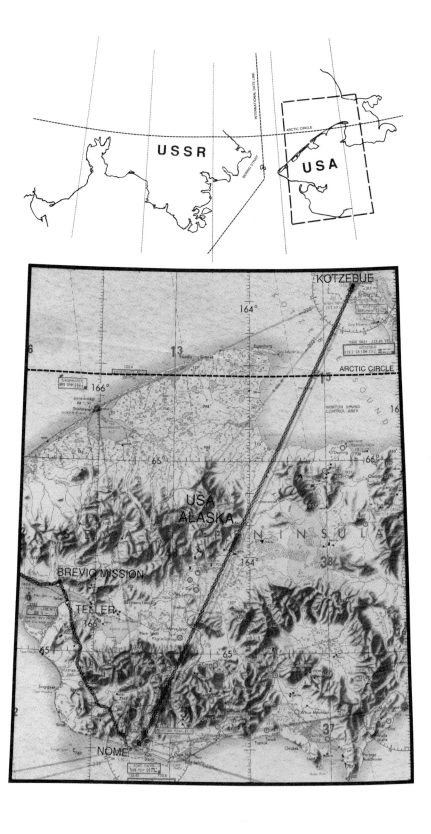

TEN

ДЕСЯТЬ

We still had hundreds of miles of Alaskan coastline to trek and many villages to visit. Thanks to the airlift from Jim Rowe, we arrived at the first village, Wales, just 20 minutes after departing Diomede early on the afternoon of Wednesday, April 26.

As Jim's Beechcraft rumbled to a halt on the snow-impacted gravel airstrip at the tiny Inupiaq village of Prince of Wales, I harbored no regrets about our decision to accept the airlift. Resorting to the use of an airplane to reach mainland Alaska cost me no pride. I was just happy to be freed from the turmoil of the Diomedes. Furthermore, the menacing wind-churned mix of ice and slush we'd seen below in the Strait as we crossed was absolutely impassable.

A few dozen villagers greeted us warmly and helped us load our supplies on sleds for the half-mile shuttle to town. A dozen high school kids lavished our huskies with affection. Dog teams are a rarity for them. The last team in this village gave way to snow machines more than 15 years ago. Though the villagers' faces reflected the strong lines of their Inupiaq heritage, their clothing—fashionable ski jackets, "moon boots" and designer sunglasses—told of their transition to the jetset world. So did their destination. These kids would be hopping on the next plane for a vacation in Hawaii.

The welcoming crowd included some familiar faces. Chief

among them was Larry Kitchener, who'd helped coordinate my planning visit here last fall. Seeing his warm toothy grin brought a broad smile to my face. Of all the non-natives I've met who have carved out a niche in the North, he stands tall as one of the most curious characters. A shaggy-haired Vietnam vet from Oklahoma, he'd moved up here years ago "to find the quiet life," he says. He ingratiated himself with the villagers and married a local woman. During my earlier visit he'd been serving an enterprising term as mayor.

"Hey, Larry, how's the hotel coming?" I shouted, nodding toward the string of bright orange portable buildings slumped on the tundra. Larry's plans called for turning these steel huts on skids, formerly towed train-like across the sea ice as housing for North Slope oil crews, into a lodge. It would serve the slow but steady stream of tourists from around the world who come here just to say they've been to the continent's end, or to make the scheduled Wednesday afternoon helicopter hop into Little Diomede to say they've gone one step farther.

Larry piled some of our load into his ramshackle yellow van, the town taxi, and led the way to the school. Stretched along a sand spit a few yards from the sea, this one-street town is a miniature mirror image of Uelen, its counterpart across the Strait. Wales too has a weather station, and on the end nearest the Strait a military outpost. Unlike the camouflaged border patrol buildings and guard tower in Uelen, this installation is a homey cluster of white clapboard buildings.

The official word has it that the civilians on duty at this Navy outpost gather only weather data, but the locals know otherwise. A submarine listening device is said to stretch from here to Fairway Rock, a pinnacle of granite that protrudes from the Strait near a deep channel just south of the Diomedes.

"When one of the kids of the Navy folks came to school one day and told us he had heard whales in his dad's office, our suspicions were pretty much confirmed," a Wales school teacher told me.

The Diomeders have their own evidence of the monitoring cable. Robert, who collects seabird eggs on Fairway Rock each spring with his relatives, says there's a small steel door along one of the cliffs.

On the other end of Wales, at the base of a natural amphitheater that rings the north and east sides of the town, is a cluster of timbers painted blue-green and draped with a web of ropes. The cluster is called "Arctic Art" and is said to represent a giant hand outstretched in friendship toward Chukotka. It was placed there by an Alaskan last year as a contribution to the many avenues being pursued to improve border relations. Soon Uelen, or some prominent point along its coastline, will boast an identical copy of the piece.

The 158 residents of Wales live in small wooden houses. Some of the homes are new three-bedroom prefabricated units, but most appear to be several decades old. Few have plumbing. As in Uelen, water for these homes is trucked in from a tundra lake and, in most, is distributed to steel holding tanks on their porches. A sewage truck collects the contents of "honey buckets" in each home.

Most homes have fuel oil heat that is supplemented by wood stoves. The nearest tree is a few hundred miles away, but the northbound currents of the Bering Sea provide this and other towns on the Seward Peninsula's south coast with a steady supply of driftwood that is washed out to sea through the Yukon Delta 200 miles to the southeast.

Chukotka doesn't have a corresponding source of fuel. The Anadyr River, the only major watershed system on the Soviet side, doesn't flow through forested lands.

The many similarities with Uelen that our Soviet teammates saw made them feel at home in Wales. In the school, though, similarities with Chukotka stopped. From its carpeted hallways and synthetic-surface gym floors to its energy-saving lighting system, the Wales school was appointed with features never found in Chukotka. Most impressive was the media room. When he saw Eskimo youngsters doing their school work on a row of Apple computers, Vadim's jaw dropped. Nothing resembling a computer is to be found in schools where he comes from. I never saw so much as a calculator in Chukotka. Tabulations are still done on an abacus.

I also had a big surprise coming. Given the number of foreign visitors reaching these Alaskan bush towns each year, I had wondered if our expedition's arrival would generate the same excitement among Alaskans as it had among Chukotkans. I worried that our Soviet friends wouldn't feel as welcomed here as we had in their homes. My concern proved needless.

The welcome was warm and wonderful. We didn't have native dances, however. Sadly, these have been all but forgotten here. Instead we were treated to that quintessentially American event—the potluck supper. Nearly all of villagers turned out in the gym with dishes in hand. Banners lined the wall with computer-generated words of welcome. We bowed our heads as an elder offered a dinner prayer, another curiosity for our Soviet friends. Then Larry started the stampede for the food line.

A buffet was spread across the rollaway tables that extended from the gym wall. The mix of native and middle-American foods elicited various responses from team members. Vadim, balancing two paper plates, passed up the roast walrus— he'd had plenty of that at home—but heaped his plate with Jell-O salad and what we in Minnesota call a macaroni "hot dish." The miniature colored marshmallows that dotted the top of dessert, a slab of devil's food cake, were no doubt the first ones he'd encountered in his life.

My favorites were the au gratin potatoes and a native food that I'd taken a liking to, the cubed pieces of beluga whale skin called muktuk. I find the pleasant taste to be faintly reminiscent of lobster.

My slides of Chukotka and our team program followed this sumptuous meal. I was as impressed as the villagers were to find that all of our Soviet friends had worked up at least part of their talks about their backgrounds in English. When their new vocabularies ran dry, Sasha served as interpreter.

Only a few of the elders in Wales remain fluent in the Inupiaq Eskimo dialect, and just two of them could understand any of the Siberian Yupik that Zoya spoke, but they were keenly attentive. Their applause and comments showed their genuine excitement about hosting Soviet guests for the first time.

The preschool children sang a series of songs that their teacher had rehearsed with them for weeks. They did their best to sing a friendship song in Russian. Then someone brought in a guitar (we had given ours to Slava, our musher companion, when he said goodbye to us in Lavrentiya), and Vadim held forth with a series of Russian ballads. The crowd was enchanted, and the kids crowded tightly around him.

The evening was far more informal and folksy than our community events in Chukotka. The effects were obvious. Our team fell in love with the town. We decided to stay the next day. Some team members spent the day visiting. Zoya was adopted by the villagers as one of their own.

A couple of townsfolk took Lonnie, Vadim and Cola on snow machine rides to an abandoned mine miles away in the tundra hills behind town. When he returned, Cola was so excited about the speed he'd experienced on an American snow machine he could hardly talk. The machines in Chukotka are much slower.

In the evening, villagers came by the school one after the other asking if they could have one of us over for dinner. We had more requests than we had team members.

The village of Wales has an endearing quality about it.

I had first felt that quality during my visit in August 1988, when I had spent four days there. My companion on that trip, a native from Teller, had introduced me to many residents. They shared their meals with me—muktuk, walrus, tundra greens and dried seal—and they shared stories of their mythology. For their ancestors, every element of the natural world had a spirit, some with special qualities. Those beliefs are no longer openly practiced, but intriguing evidence of them still exists in Wales.

One example is the Rainbow Rock. When our expedition was in Wales, the rock was buried in snow drifts, but in August when I was there, this bright white boulder, as tall as an adult and lodged on a hillside a mile behind town, was clearly visible against the russet brown tundra moss. Its whiteness struck me as highly unusual. I asked one of the village elders about it. "Oh, that's just paint," he said with a laugh.

His comment piqued my curiosity even more. Why would anyone want to paint the rock? Well, the elder explained, years ago a rainbow of light would extend from that rock over the town and into the sea. The light appeared for a brief moment at every sunrise and sunset for as long as anyone could remember. But then, he said, sometime around World War II it stopped. The military built an airstrip then and staffed a small defense installation. The villagers assumed that the military activities disrupted the Rainbow Rock. The rusting hulks of landing craft can still be seen on the beach.

When the war ended and the military ceased most operations here, the villagers waited for the light to return. When it didn't, one man decided to act. He found several cans of white paint in the abandoned barracks and dumped them on the rock. "Somehow he thought that making it real bright and shiny might bring it back to life," the elder explained.

The elder also told me of another bit of evidence of the old beliefs. "While you're here, you should hike up to the hilltop and see the mukluk prints in the stone," he said. "They say they were put there when the earth was still young and soft."

That's all it took. That same afternoon, I clambered up to the crest overlooking the town. There on an anvil-shaped slab of rock I found them— a series of child-size footprints. Most were weathered and barely discernible, but one was distinct. It was about a half-inch deep into the granite. The edges were faintly ribbed, suggesting the puckering found where the sole of a mukluk is turned up.

Our visit to Wales with the expedition allowed no further sightseeing for me. I spent most of our layover day on the telephone, making plans for the miles ahead. We got some bad news. The crisp, clear, zero-degree day we enjoyed here in Wales was a far cry from the weather just a hundred miles eastward. Temperatures there were pushing past the melting point. It was raining in Nome. Though there was still some three feet of snow on the ground, that would soon be turning to slush.

The fickle weather of the Bering region, which had been a controlling factor through so much of this journey, would have the final word. We had to shorten our route. We could make it to the villages of Brevig Mission and Teller, 60 miles eastward, but it would take a bit of luck and a break in the rain to be able to ski the additional 80 miles to Nome. Trail conditions were tough. Snow machines were bogging down in three feet of slush, and mushers had all but given up on the season and put away their sleds.

We had no hope of continuing our journey beyond Nome.

The many river crossings on our route would be impassable. Meltwater surging through the rivers would overflow onto the surface ice and inundate the surrounding areas.

Cutting the route short wasn't just a matter of missing some miles. Hanging up our skis in Nome also meant missing several settlements on our original itinerary. Golovin, Council, White Mountain, Elim, Koyuk, Buckland and Deering—dots on our map that held much interest for all of us— would all be dropped. This development was a bitter disappointment for me. Many of their residents are Yupik Eskimos who should surely be tied into the bridge.

Fortunately, with a few more phone calls I found that Alaska Airlines was willing to airlift us to our final destination of Kotzebue. This city on the north side of the Seward Peninsula was a key stop. For one, it's Ernie's hometown. It's also the largest Eskimo settlement in the U.S. Eighty-five percent of its 3,500 residents are native. Even though we wouldn't get to as many western Alaska settlements as we had hoped, we could still extend the message of our journey to the vast majority of the region's residents.

The team accepted these changes with mixed feelings. We were already several weeks behind schedule. Many team members had families and jobs to get back to. Nonetheless, we had looked forward to visiting nearly as many communities in Alaska as we had in Chukotka, and our Soviet friends were upset that their U.S. visit would be curtailed. We'd spent nearly two months in their country, but they would have only a few weeks in ours.

To reciprocate we made plans to travel as a team across the U.S. after the expedition. In one frantic day of phone calls in Wales, Ginna and I arranged an itinerary that would take us to Anchorage; Seattle; Minneapolis, and Duluth, Minnesota; and New York. Sponsors offered to help arrange sightseeing and community appearances for the team in each city.

Weeks before in Chukotka, Dmitry had put plans in motion for two planeloads of Soviets to meet us for a celebration in Alaska upon completion of the trek. The event was set for May 10 in Kotzebue. Another flurry of calls was needed to get U.S.

State Department approval for Aeroflot planes to enter U.S. air space. We faced some technical hurdles on this matter, but the fact that the U.S. and Soviet governments cooperated was clear evidence that the defections had not taken a serious toll on border relations.

The stress of the defections together with the crossing difficulties and our entry into the U.S. had changed our team dynamics. For one thing the passing of the organizational baton lifted some of Dmitry's load and added to mine. That loss of control left him noticeably irritable. He sparred with me about the order of events for our community program. "We give talk first then you show slides," he insisted.

I let it go. It was understandably difficult for him to no longer be master of ceremonies.

He and I had learned how to prove a point with an annoying jab. Like rival siblings we had learned how to push each other's buttons. In the give and take of our relationship as co-leaders this generally caused no harm, though. Rather it served to identify issues that stood between us.

That morning, for example, following our breakfast in the gym, I called a quick huddle of the American team members to discuss the financing of our tour across the U.S. Because the topic didn't require input from our Soviet friends, there was no reason to involve them. I asked Dmitry if they, in the meantime, would be willing to clear the breakfast dishes from the tables. Yes, he nodded, and they set to work. A few minutes later I noticed they were about to leave with half the dishes still in place. "What about the rest of them?" I asked Dmitry.

"Those are the Americans' dishes," he said with a mock smile. It was his way of letting me know that if I made a distinction between our American and Soviet team members then so would he. No lengthy discussion was needed on such topics anymore. Just a quick jab made the point.

Being in a pressure-cooker setting during the past couple of weeks had also had a bonding influence on all 12 of us. Like soldiers coming off the battlefield we had shared a depth of experience that gave us a glimpse of each other's souls. We still weren't one big happy family, but we had a much better idea of who we were traveling with. Few pretenses or polite facades cluttered our conversations anymore. Communication obstacles still crippled our team meetings, but we were now better able to at least get the drift of each other's comments. Subtle shades of gray had replaced the blacks and whites in which our understanding of each other had been painted.

For example, my relationship with Cola was no longer defined by our differing opinions about how close his dogs should be allowed to other dogs or people. To be sure, I was still unhappy with his cavalier handling of his team. We'd suffered another incident. A boy had been nipped in Diomede. Fortunately the wound was minor, and Cola was making an effort to isolate his animals. In Wales he kept them out at the airstrip, so we set the issue aside. As a result, for the first time in weeks we found ourselves sharing laughter more often than exchanging icy glares.

Though the journey was winding down, camaraderie was still important for our success and safety. In fact, the next day, the weather tested our togetherness.

As we left Wales, blustery north winds trapped us in a whirl of white. By early afternoon the winds had grown into steady gales. Struggling to hit their stride on our first full day on skis in nearly two weeks, team members were spread up and down the coast. With visibility dropping steadily, the situation was unnerving.

Dmitry shuffled along in the rear. We found ourselves waiting time and again for him to catch up. Our frustration mounted. So did his. On one occasion when Dmitry caught up, he laid into Vadim, our front-runner, for striking too brisk a pace. In an unusual display of anger, Dmitry raked Vadim up and down in front of the other team members.

It seemed unfair. I felt Dmitry should speed up rather than demand that Vadim slow down. The rest of us were having no trouble staying right behind Vadim.

Now it was my turn to launch a little jab. I suggested to Dmitry that he tow behind one of the dog sleds. "When you ski," I said, "all people must wait."

Pushing that button worked. It left Dmitry sullen for a long time, but he managed to ski along with us.

Later that afternoon the winds roared to a crescendo. I had

never seen anything like it. Fully loaded sleds were toppled by the gusts. People were knocked down time and again, and the dogs veered downwind to escape the blast. It was pointless to try to communicate with anyone. We just followed whatever dark blur was moving ahead. With one hand we'd stick a ski pole in the snow to prop ourselves up so we could scratch away at frosted goggles and glasses with the other hand to maintain some visibility.

We were putting out a tremendous amount of energy and making virtually no headway. Before long we were thoroughly separated. The dark blur that I was following turned out to be Alexander. When we reached a protected bay where we could talk, I learned that he hadn't seen any dark blurs in front of him for a long time. I figured that most if not all of the crew was still behind us. Sooner or later—if they didn't veer out toward the open sea—they would pass through this same sheltered bay. We lay down in a crag in the rocks to wait.

An hour passed. Then, one by one, six of our teammates turned up. The others, we soon learned, were waiting just ahead. Everyone was safe, but we all knew we had courted disaster. It was time to tighten up once again.

We reached Brevig Mission, a village of 160 Inupiaq Eskimos, in two days of travel. The teachers, all non-natives, put on a spaghetti feed for us and our program drew a large, enthusiastic crowd. Hosting their first Soviet guests was a great source of excitement for them.

Although Wales had been a special stop for our Eskimo team members, Brevig held a unique interest for Vadim and Cola, our Chukchi members. Brevig is the birthplace of western Alaska's reindeer herding industry. Though no Chukchi now reside here or anywhere else in Alaska, a few of them were among Brevig's first residents. Many villages on both sides of the Strait evolved late in the last century as semi-nomadic clusters of native people settled near trading posts, missions or government offices. Brevig took shape around a mission established by Olaf Brevig, a Norwegian immigrant.

Brevig's claim to fame as the birthplace of the reindeer industry resulted from the efforts of Sheldon Jackson, pioneer missionary and General Agent for Education in Alaska. His observations led him to conclude that the Eskimos needed a new source of protein. Though Jackson's judgments were later deemed wrong, he felt that seriously depleted stocks of walrus, whales and caribou threatened the native population with starvation.

Reasoning that reindeer could provide a more stable food source, he sailed to Chukotka in 1892 and returned with 171 reindeer. Also on board were a handful of Chukchi herders, who had been hired to teach their skills to the Eskimos in Brevig. The reindeer flourished in Alaska, but the Chukchi didn't. For reasons not clearly understood they simply didn't get along with the local Eskimos. Two years later they returned home.

To replace them the enterprising Jackson brought in Lapp herders from Scandinavia. He also imported more stock, and by the time the Russia's czarist government banned such trade in 1902, more than a thousand Chukotkan reindeer had been delivered to the Brevig area.

The herds expanded rapidly, and by 1914 all grazing land in the region was divided up between herds. As Jackson had envisioned, the reindeer became a well-liked food source for the Eskimos. The meat proved even more important for the population boom the Seward Peninsula experienced during its turn-of-the-century gold rush.

As the boom gave out, so did the reindeer market. By 1930 the dwindling herds were consolidated and turned over to village cooperatives. Ironically, these were organized much like the collective farms in Chukotka, though there was no contact between the communities at that time. By 1951 the herds had experienced a catastrophic decline, due to disease and overgrazing, and just 6,500 animals remained.

Today Eskimo herders in the region look after about 16,000 animals. With demand outstripping production, there is much interest in bolstering the industry. Some Alaskans are looking across the Strait for help. The Chukotkans currently manage 10 times as many animals as do the villagers in western Alaska.

With help from Ginna, the Alaskan governor's office is considering various proposals for securing additional breed stock and herd management information from Chukotka. In return,

Alaska can offer meat-processing technology. Alaska might also serve as a conduit for Chukotka to gain access to overseas markets.

Any means of boosting the reindeer industry and providing some source of community identity would be welcomed by Brevig. In the estimation of many community leaders, this village, like others in western Alaska, is languishing. Cultural traditions are eroding fast. The schools, which in decades past sought to eradicate the native languages, have since launched campaigns to preserve them. In most Inupiaq villages, the native tongue is rarely spoken in the homes except among the elders. One study predicts that Inupiaq won't be spoken by the year 2020. The Yupik language is still strong among Darlene's neighbors on St. Lawrence but there, too, shows signs of decline.

Subsistence lifestyles, a cornerstone of Eskimo culture even after the people settled in villages, are no longer embraced by young people. Virtually no jobs are available to them. One source of cash they commonly resort to is the sale of fossilized ivory. During summer months, many villagers dig down through the middens—the heaps of soil containing the layered remnants of their ancestors' homes—to find ancient carvings or ivory workings such as harpoon heads, dolls and whole walrus tusks, stained brown from centuries in the soil. Some villagers decry selling their heritage, but the lucrative prices available from ivory traders make this quick source of cash irresistible to many.

Family structure is deteriorating. Teen-age pregnancies are common. One pastor in Brevig told me that he has baptized children in the past two years but has performed no marriages. The last marriage in his church took place in 1981.

Alcohol abuse is rampant. Even though most of the villages, like Brevig, have been officially declared "dry," booze finds it way in. So do drugs, in alarming amounts. I was told that it is not at all uncommon to see young people openly dealing in marijuana and cocaine in the village. Often the booze and drugs are smuggled in by ivory traders who arrive by bush plane and trade the substances directly for fossilized carvings.

"They're selling their cultural soul for substances that destroy their bodies and their lives," said a teacher.

In Chukotka, on the other hand, a drug problem does not yet exist. Alcoholism, though apparent in some Chukotkan villages, is controlled in part by the fact that distribution difficulties and strict quotas limit the amount of booze that makes it to that remote corner of the Soviet Union.

The demise of native cultures appears to be occurring far less rapidly in Chukotka. The people there express the same concerns about loss of the native languages as the Alaskans do, but efforts in Chukotka to preserve native dances and art are far better organized.

Perhaps the most important factor is that subsistence life-style activities have been integrated into the village economies. Fishing, caribou herding and sea mammal hunting have been adapted directly and are controlled on a sustainable basis. The fox farms and reindeer herds tap native skills in animal husbandry. Cooperatives for producing art and native skin clothing yield marketable products while preserving skills. This network of enterprises—the Chukotkan version of the Soviet collective farm—assures native villagers a livelihood in which they can take much pride and which will lend their communities a cultural identity. That may sound like Soviet propaganda, but my observations supported it.

Despite their economic differences, the villages in Chukotka and Alaska were remarkably similar in the enthusiasm they demonstrated for our expedition. In a scene reminiscent of our send-off from Lavrentiya, school children in Brevig escorted us on skis to Teller, just eight miles away across a large bay. They stayed with us even as the heavy clouds oozed with a steady drizzle.

A cluster of villagers, many of them relatives or close acquaintances of Ernie and Robert, cheered our arrival and led us into the school, where a Sunday afternoon potluck feast was held in our honor. It was April 30, Alexander's birthday. Later that evening we celebrated with a team party in the school cafeteria.

During the layover team members offered programs at the school and dispersed to visit with townsfolk.

A few of us were battling a touch of snow blindness. Despite our use of sunglasses, the unbroken mantle of white we had faced during each day of travel on the tundra had taken its toll. I got hit the worst. I covered my face with a dark kerchief to rest my eyes. With a few days rest, the retinas—burned out by over exposure—healed up. The condition is excruciating. Each time I moved my eyes while they were healing, it felt like coarse sandpaper had been rubbed across my eyeballs. Snow blindness can also be quite dangerous. Repeated occurrences can lead to permanent eye damage.

The weather remained rotten as we left Teller on a 70-mile overland journey to Nome. We would be lucky to get there on skis. Our faces glistened with mist. Though most of the tundra still had ample snow cover, we often had to skid across patches of exposed ground.

In another scene reminiscent of our experiences in Chukotka, we enjoyed the help and company of a local native musher that day. Joe Garney, a renowned sled dog racer, toted some of our gear with his team and visited with us at our camp that evening.

The next day drizzle dampened our clothes and our spirits. The soft sticky snow tugged at our skis and sleds. By mid-afternoon the drizzle had let up, but some trail-weary teammates campaigned for calling it a day and setting camp. I convinced them that the only way to fight a chill was to keep moving. I argued that our dampened synthetic garments would dry quickly as our bodies pumped heat through them. We squeezed a few more hours and miles out of the day.

We camped along the road near a river crossing about 25 miles shy of Nome. Anne Walker reported by radio from our base that the townspeople and school children had planned a special welcoming ceremony for us the next day. Please be there by three, Anne asked. To keep that schedule we were up at five and under way by seven. We slogged toward town, sometimes plodding through deep pools of meltwater. Often our skis got sucked down into slush.

Our soggy arrival was hardly the triumphant finale we had hoped for. Nonetheless, after enduring more snow and sleet, we managed to limp into Nome on time. A huge throng awaited us on the wharf, where the city's business center joins the seafront. Balloons and banners brightened the gray day.

Journalists cornered us. How do you feel? they asked.

"Just happy to be here," I said as I raked a clump of sleet from my beard.

Community leaders took to the podium on an old ore wagon and showered our team with greetings. Then we took our place on the wagon and, standing arm in arm with the Soviet and American flags stretched side by side in front of us, we posed for team photos. An opening cleared in the crowd in front of us, and the town's native dance company stepped forward to perform. As we watched the dancers' hands gracefully scribe the air and we felt the strong rhythm of the skin drums, we looked at each other and smiled. These familiar dances, echoes through time, had come to symbolize for us the link our trek was helping to forge between the natives on both sides of the border.

We spent four bustling days in Nome. We gave programs for the schools and swapped mushing stories at a reception hosted by members of the local kennel club. We also underwent a final battery of medical tests administered by two members of the Soviet research team. These men had secured visas allowing them to arrive in Little Diomede with the Soviet delegation and then stay on in Alaska until we concluded our trek.

The tremendous interest the people in Nome showed in our project and the support they generated for it was gratifying. The *Nome Nugget*, the town's weekly newspaper, carried front page stories on our progress in nearly every issue while we were on our trek. The two radio stations, KNOM and KICY, covered us regularly and sent stories on to networks.

The highlight of our visit to Nome was a community banquet on Saturday night, our final evening there. Following the meal we gave an abbreviated version of our community program.

The crowd was intrigued with our slides, but what moved them most were Dmitry's comments. Alaska and Chukotka, he said, will play an increasingly important role in Soviet-American relations. The efforts of people in Nome are helping to ensure that. This city, he added, has become the window through which the people of Chukotka view the warmth and friendship in the hearts of American people. The crowd responded to Dmitry with a standing ovation.

The next day we flew to Kotzebue, our last stop. The people of this community had a new hometown hero, Ernie, among us, and they had gone to great lengths to prepare a special welcome. The school band, standing on the airport tarmac, performed the Soviet and American national anthems for us as we disembarked. On the street in front of the terminal a parade awaited us. We took our places among the fire trucks and ambulances festooned with banners and balloons and marched into town as sirens blared around us. Willie Hensley, a former state senator and one of Alaska's most prominent native leaders, hosted a banquet for our team and leaders from the community that evening. There Ernie was honored for having represented the spirit of Kotzebue throughout our journey.

Meanwhile preparations were under way to host the Soviets who were due to arrive from Chukotka on two Aeroflot planes. Though they had been expected on Monday, paperwork delayed their arrival until Wednesday, May 10.

As the approach of these two Soviet airplanes into Kotzebue was announced, our team lined up on the tarmac with business and government officials. The two 40-passenger planes landed, and after customs formalities the 76 passengers filed past us. Many familiar faces were among them. Nicolai Kashtikin, the Chukotkan leader from Anadyr, came by first and greeted us each with a warm hug. His inspiring comments upon our send-off in March about how the people of Chukotka would be traveling with us all of the way now had more meaning than ever. Also among the Soviet guests were members of Dmitry's support staff and leaders from many of the villages we had traveled through. The event became an unexpectedly joyous rendezvous. Perhaps the warmest hugs were exchanged with Slava Practina, the cheery Yupik musher who had been our companion through much of our travels in Chukotka.

The entourage was transported to the high school gym, where a full-fledged Soviet-American pep rally was under way, led by cheerleaders and the high school band. As the Soviet delegation filed in, a tumultuous roar of applause erupted from the hundreds of townspeople in the bleachers. The Soviets in turn beamed with delight and waved energetically.

More songs and cheers followed, and then the ceremony began. Accolades and gifts were heaped on the Soviet leaders and our team by local and state officials for nearly two hours. Among the letters read was one from Alaska's Governor Cowper. He wrote, in part, "Your expedition is admirable, not only for the physical exertion and logistics required but for your significant contribution to improving relations between Alaska and the Soviet Union. One of your goals was to advance world peace, and toward that end I believe you have taken a giant step forward."

Then Willie Hensley read a telegram that had been received that day. This telegram meant as much to us as the one we had received weeks earlier from General Secretary Gorbachev.

This new telegram was from the White House and President George Bush:

> Crossing more than 1,000 miles and the treacherous waters of the Bering Strait, your journey has been a remarkable demonstration of human strength and stamina. But more important, it has reminded us of the close ties which unite the Eskimo peoples on both sides of the Strait. You can be proud of your role in helping to strengthen those ties. In their official orders dated January 2, 1719, the Russian explorers Fedor Luzhin and Ivan Evreinov were told to answer the question: 'Are America and Asia joined?' Thanks to your efforts, this 270-year-old question can be answered, 'yes.' May God bless you always.

A Kotzebue village elder named Alfred Wells offered the final and perhaps most poignant words of the program. Addressing the Soviet guests, he said, "This past year you helped us search for hunters lost at sea near St. Lawrence Island, you've helped us rescue the whales stranded near Barrow and now you're helping us clean up our oil spill in Prudhoe Bay. What can we do for you in return? I wish I could give more, but the only thing I have to offer you is my love."

With the speech-giving complete, the grade school choir

sang songs in Inupiaq and Russian. Then the community dancers performed and managed to draw most of the crowd, including the Soviet leaders and our team members, onto the gym floor to join them for the last two Eskimo dances.

Even Kashtikin caught the beat. I hadn't expected this expedition to lead to an opportunity to shuck and jive alongside the First Secretary of Chukotka's Communist Party, but then it had held many surprises for me.

When the dancing was finished, Dmitry and I pulled two of our expedition dog sleds out to the center of the floor. We invited everyone to autograph the fabric covers on each sled. We explained that the sleds would be presented as mementos of our expedition to museums in each country. We laid out a set of colored markers they could write with, and the crowd responded enthusiastically.

The State Department authorization for the Soviets' visit had stipulated a duration of six hours. The Soviet planes were allowed to be parked on the Kotzebue airstrip from 10:00 a.m to 4:00 p.m, the same time frame in which Alaska Airlines had visited Anadyr to deliver our American team, but the afternoon ceremony lasted far longer than planned.

When it became apparent that the Soviet delegation would overstay the designated time, Alaskan Airlines officials who had joined us for the event put an appeal through by phone to Washington for an extension. Fortunately, they happened upon a sympathetic State Department staffer who granted an immediate extension.

At six, we all went back to the airstrip. The Soviet expedition equipment and sled dogs were loaded onto the planes. Slava Practina would look after the dogs while Cola and Vadim continued on with us for our tour across the U.S. One of our sleds, now covered in signatures in English and Russian, was also loaded on the plane.

Then one more short ceremony took place. Seated at a table on the tarmac, officials from Chukotka and Kotzebue signed a protocol that specified goals for the development of trade and tourism relations between this city and communities across the Strait. There was one last flurry of picture taking and hugs as the Soviets boarded their planes. They waved from the windows as the hatches were closed.

But then there was one more surprise. As we stood by to see the Soviets off, waiting for the pilots to start and warm up the engines, we heard a sputter and a cough and then a steady clicking. The noise was familiar, especially to a couple of Minnesotans who know the rigors of starting a car in the dead of winter. "Doesn't that sound like a dead battery to you?" I asked Lonnie. He nodded. It was.

The pilots in the other plane tried to start their engines. The response was the same. They climbed down and examined the electrical cables under a panel in the wing. It was clear that the batteries had simply gone dead while sitting for nearly 10 hours in 20-degree weather. An airplane mechanic explained that it isn't uncommon for that to happen. Large planes generally require a jump start if they've been sitting for long, but the charger at the airport was the wrong size for the Soviet batteries.

Word went out around town that help was needed. Soon mechanics arrived to offer their assistance—tools, batteries and jumper cables in hand. I watched this amazing vignette of cross-cultural cooperation from a window in the terminal building. The local tire jockeys in their baseball caps, and Soviet pilots in long woolen coats with polished brass buttons searched for solutions. Finally one of their efforts worked. Some new connection of cables allowed them to give a boost to the motors. With a burst of smoke an engine roared to life. Soon all were revving. Minutes later we waved goodbye, and the planes soared westward over the Strait.

Just as it began, the trek ended in a howling blizzard.

Another warm welcome.

The Soviets issued a commemorative stamp in honor of the Bering Bridge Expedition.

With the departure of the Soviet planes from Kotzebue on that Wednesday evening, May 10, the expedition was over, but our travel certainly wasn't. The 12 of us hardly had time to catch our breath before we launched a blitz across the U.S.

The post-expedition whirlwind swept us on to Anchorage, Seattle, Minneapolis and Duluth, and then on to New York City.

Our Seattle visit included a party at a historical museum with donors sipping champagne in a garden awash in the sweet strains of a harp. But the highlight of the stop was a raucous waterfront disco that was complete with a fog machine, MTV on floor-to-ceiling screens, laser lights and pulsating colored strobes. We went there at Zoya's insistence. After spending hours cramped in airplanes, her dancing legs needed some action. She bought a silky, lime green floral blouse and matching pedal-pushers for the occasion. "We dance now," she said to me as soon as we went through the establishment's suede-covered doors. Dance we did, until I nearly dropped. When we left, after four hours, she was radiant and I was beat.

The next stop, Minnesota, was a homecoming for Lonnie and me.

We stepped off the jetway in Minneapolis and were greeted with hugs, flowers and banners. My little daughter Bria was a hit again. "Ya hachoo soupa," she shouted out to our Soviet teammates, speaking the one Russian phrase she knew. They burst into laughter. This, the first sentence in my Russian lesson book, means "I want soup."

In Red Wing, the Mississippi River town where Susan grew up, a special event awaited us. Sponsors hosted a party on a paddle-wheel boat with a Dixieland band. The warm breezes and verdant landscape swept memories of arctic snowstorms from our minds. For our Soviet team members in particular, the Mississippi River experience was a dream come true. It brought to life for them scenes from stories of one of their favorite authors, Mark Twain.

The next day we piled in vans and traveled up the state to reach the port city of Duluth, Minnesota, on the western tip of Lake Superior. Lonnie and I watched as our teammates' eyes opened wide when they saw ocean-going ships harbored smack in the center of the continent.

"How can that be?" Vadim asked me with a look of puzzlement.

"The city put them there as a tourist attraction," I quipped in return before explaining the intricacies and the reach of the St. Lawrence Seaway.

In Duluth we once again enjoyed a potluck dinner in a church basement. Our Soviet team members had been turned on to Jell-O salads and "hot dish" in Alaska and once again emptied the bowls on the buffet table. "I like marshmallows," Alexander said between bites.

We had been on a high for several days, albeit a harried one, and our energy built to a peak that evening. The 700 folks attending our program in a Duluth high school got an earful from us—three hours' worth. Each of us added a few gems to the usual patter. Dmitry noted that the National Guard chaplain who offered a prayer to open the event was the first evidence he had seen of the military in America. Cola offered a joke. He noted dryly that his name had been misspelled on the program and that the same mistake had been made on printed materials at other stops. "To make it easier for my new American friends, I will simply change the way I spell my name," he said.

Team members were so enchanted by their visit to Minnesota that some of us, Soviets and Americans alike, joked among ourselves that we might face a few more defections.

The fun faded when we hit our last stop, New York. A couple of days there left everyone longing for home. For one thing, we hit the Big Apple on the down side. By this point on our race across the States, we were emotionally and physically drained. The city, crazed and crowded as always, stood in sharp contrast to the relatively tranquil stops along our tour. The headlines in *The New York Times* on the morning after our arrival didn't help. One announced that a rapist was loose in the hotel we were staying in. Another told of a murder that had occurred in a nearby restaurant, only hours after we had finished dining there the night before.

"Get me out of here!" Robert said to me that morning as he battled a wave of homesickness.

The lump of rock that he lives on at the edge of the Arctic Circle was starting to seem mighty appealing to me, too.

Nonetheless, our visit had its bright moments, including a team photo session in Central Park. On our last evening, we gathered in a hotel room to exchange gifts and toasts with Russian vodka. The gifts included an expedition poster featuring portrait illustrations of each team member. I had arranged for the poster to be produced in Minnesota while we were on the trail. From Dmitry we received small cloth banners emblazoned with the Soviet expedition logo. It featured stylized drawings of an American and Soviet Eskimo with hands raised and joined in celebration.

The same logo appeared on a Soviet postage stamp that Alexander gave us. We learned that the Soviet government had issued the commemorative stamp to honor our trek. A supply of these stamps and the banners had been given to our Soviet teammates by the Soviet delegation that had visited Kotzebue for our closing ceremonies.

We treasured the stamps as if they were gold medals. The stamps and the messages we received from President Bush and General Secretary Gorbachev were clear evidence that our expedition had had a positive influence on the people of Alaska and Chukotka and on the governments of both countries.

The day after our farewell party, our Soviet teammates flew to Moscow as the rest of us returned home to Alaska and Minnesota.

In the months that followed, the Bering Bridge Expedition continued to preoccupy many of us. The journey certainly captured media attention. Stories appeared in magazines and newspapers throughout the world, and *National Geographic* television produced a film for the *Explorer* series. Many films and articles were produced in the Soviet Union, too.

The major follow-up to the Bering Bridge Expedition has not been media coverage, however, but, appropriately enough, the multitude of people-to-people meetings that spun off in its wake.

In that light, Dmitry and I were determined to set the example of continuing communication and understanding by examining the complications of our own relationship. The ordeals we had slogged through together on the trail had left our deep mutual respect intact. Our difficulties had been severe enough to drive us apart, but to allow that to happen would have been to forsake the basic mission of the expedition. We chose, therefore, to continue to work hard at the task of understanding each other and to find ways to appreciate our differences.

After a month's respite from our trip, Dmitry and I renewed communications. In an exchange of direct and thoughtful letters, we worked at ironing out our differences point by point. We recognized that most of our conflicts had arisen from communications obstacles and that our most profound differences had far more to do with personality than culture. Dmitry, the seasoned pragmatist, and Paul, the young brash idealist, had simply locked horns when those qualities clashed. We also recognized that our personalities had often complemented each other nicely.

As co-leaders we had persevered with our relationship long enough and worked through our struggles well enough to build our own bridges.

Meanwhile, in the Bering region itself, the bridge was being reconstructed at a breathtaking pace. The depth and variety of events was simply astounding. Every time I called friends in Alaska, I learned that something new was in the works. It was difficult to keep track of the developments that continued to

PAUL
Emissary of change

occur, linking communities on both sides of the Strait during the summer of 1989.

Beyond any doubt the bridge is open:

In mid-September, officials from Washington and Moscow ratified the agreement called for in the protocol that Governor Kobets and Governor Cowper signed upon our team's crossing of the U.S.-Soviet border. Natives of the Bering region in both countries can now traverse the Strait without visas. Certain restrictions apply, but for Yupik and Inupiaq people, the crossroads of continents no longer has a roadblock in the center.

Our expedition team members, some from afar and others close at hand, watched these developments with amazement and pride. Many of these breakthroughs might have happened without our journey, but we know that at the very least we hastened the day of their arrival.

Back home in Minnesota I savored a hot summer with Susan and Bria in the north woods. We savored as well the fact that the dream had come true. We had played a role in focusing the attention of our governments on the bridge.

The 12 citizen diplomats of our expedition had positively influenced Soviet-American relations. We had done our part to help relegate the Cold War to the dust bin of history.

The Bering Bridge Expedition, a journey born of personal vision, highly ambitious and idealistic, had reached its goal despite the hardships of high adventure and communications obstacles that might have crippled us.

We had met tension and strife. We had dealt with shattered expectations. We had sometimes sparred over minor issues that took on significance only in the pressure-cooker setting of an

217

ordeal. Our heated exchanges never came to blows, but our goodwill and patience were at times severely tested.

We also enjoyed the startling transitions from expedition tensions to excitement and warmth in visits to remote settlements along our route.

One element above all others bonded us:

Though we didn't always feel it out there on the trail, we were on a mission. Each of us wanted to help the people of our two countries learn to live and work in peace. Our expedition was a living, working metaphor for the hope that we shared. We were emissaries of change.

Arranged events for the benefit of the press went sour. Fickle and furious weather jarred our plans. Defections, we feared, might even derail the trek. But through it all we established powerful human connections, and we had helped bring two nations together.

During our trip, our Soviet-American team crossed the International Date Line. In one short step we passed from Asia to North America, from the Soviet Union to the United States. In that same small step we also made a passage through time, stepping from Monday back into Sunday, from tomorrow into today.

For us, this time change held symbolic significance because in many ways the members of our 12-person team could truly say that we have seen tomorrow. We have seen a tomorrow when the people of our two countries will learn, just as we have learned, that the strength of common goals can outweigh cultural and political differences. We have seen a tomorrow when shared challenges will forge bonds among diverse peoples.

Our experiences on the Bering Bridge Expedition provided an example for us of how this transition will take place for all people.

On our first day on the trail we embarked on a thousand-mile expedition as 12 virtual strangers. We were knit loosely together only by the vague notion that maybe, just maybe, this project would make a difference.

Indeed, it did for us and for a great many other people. Along the way our team became something of a family. We overcame many physical adversities and language barriers. We shared fatigue, fears, laughter and joy and a profound sense of gratification.

This journey didn't end when we reached our destination in Kotzebue, Alaska. This journey will continue throughout our lives until the tomorrow that we glimpsed on our expedition becomes today for all Soviet and American people.

The Bering Bridge helped open the road to peace, a road we can walk all our lives.

TEAM MEMBERS

PAUL SCHURKE. Paul developed a love for wild places early on when his mother and father, a homemaker/teacher and building inspector/carpenter, respectively, purchased property on a river in northern Wisconsin. Roaming those woods and waterways and early forays into Minnesota's Boundary Waters Canoe Area locked in his passion for adventure. That, coupled with the Benedictine influences of his college, St. John's University, led a classmate and Paul to establish Wilderness Inquiry, an adventure program for physically disabled people.

At their wilderness home, Paul and his wife, Susan, operate a winter ski treks program and cold-weather apparel design business. While Susan produces and markets Eskimo-style garments from modern materials, Paul coordinates winter wilderness excursions by dog sled and ski for community, college and business groups.

For information contact: Wintergeen, Ely, Minnesota 55731.

DMITRY SHPARO. Dmitry grew up in Moscow during World War II. In 1969, during his second year of college, he went on his first expedition, a ski trek across a tundra lake in the western Soviet arctic. The experience was miserable physically but mentally exhilarating. It led him to launch a series of long ski treks in the arctic and polar regions almost every year since.

Dmitry looks every bit the part of a polar explorer and, exuding confidence and directness, is a born leader and diplomat as well. A man of many moods, his face flashes from a cold, penetrating steely gaze to heart-melting charm and affection in a second. He is determined that his next trek take him across Antartica on skis.

LONNIE DUPRE. Lonnie is a wiry, black bearded, native of Chisago City, Minnesota. He has always had an affinity for northern adventure.

He has read about polar explorers since he was a kid, led winter camping trips in Minnesota's Boundary Waters Canoe

Area and lived in Alaska for three years. In Alaska he worked as a commercial fisherman and as a carpenter.

In 1984, while he was on a 10-week camping and snowshoe jaunt in the remote reaches of Alaska's Brooks Range, his passion for the north fixed on a dream—he became determined to complete the first solo trek from the North Pole to Oodaq Island, Greenland, a gravel bar that represents the northernmost chunk of real estate in the world.

GINNA BRELSFORD. Ginna is blonde, blue-eyed and an exceptionally good cross-country skier. She was dubbed "Snow White" by one article in the Soviet press.

Her academic and professional credentials are more than a match for any storybook character. She received undergraduate degrees in world religions and international development from Brown University and a master's degree from Fletcher School of Law and Diplomacy. In the years since she has served the Alaska State Legislature as an administrative assistant, the Municipality of Anchorage as an economic developer and, currently, the Alaskan governor's Office of International Trade, as coordinator of the governor's Soviet initiatives.

Her efforts are now focused on the coordination of an International Northern Regions Conference in Anchorage in 1990. The conference will include many Soviet delegates. Ginna returned to Chutkotka in the fall of 1989 with a delegation to continue her work on trade relations.

ROBERT SOOLOOK JR.. Robert is one of a family of 10 children. He lost his father when he was young but learned hunting and fishing skills from the elders in his Inupiaq Eskimo village of Little Diomede.

Between hunting, fishing and crabbing seasons, he works in the village gym, where he has gained legendary skills as a basketball player.

In 1985, Robert, like many of the young men in his village, joined the First Scout Battalion of the Alaskan National Guard. As part of his Guard duties, he maintains "spotting reports" on Soviet activities on Big Diomede Island.

When Paul first met him on Little Diomede in August 1988,

Robert was dutifully recording the sighting of a Soviet fishing vessel.

Two months after completion of the Bering Bridge Expedition, Robert hopped on a Soviet skin boat passing his island en route to Alaska. The Chukotkan team members of this "Penguin" expedition were on a three-week goodwill tour of Seward Peninsula communities.

ERNIE NORTON. Ernie, who was called the "human skiing machine" by the team, is a quiet man who proved often to be a pace setter.

Born in the tiny Inupiaq Eskimo settlement of Noatak and raised in Kotzebue, Ernie secured a degree from the University of Alaska-Fairbanks. He majored in secondary education with minors in anthropology and archeology.

He has begun his graduate studies on the anthropology of the Bering Region at the Center for Northern Studies, Wolcott, Vermont. He plans to complete them at the University of California-Berkeley.

He makes his livelihood as a commercial salmon fisherman in summer and a high school teacher in winter.

DARLENE APANGALOOK. Darlene learned to speak both Siberian Yupik and English as child in her home town of Gambell on St. Lawrence Island, a village of 500 that is one of the most traditional Eskimo settlements in Alaska.

A few of the elders in her community were born in Chukotka, and her family is aware of dozens of relatives still living there. Her father is full-bloodied Yupik, and her mother is Klinkit Indian and Norwegian.

Darlene, whose Eskimo name is Komlena, has completed three years of college studies toward an interdisciplinary studies degree from the University of Alaska-Anchorage. She returned to Chukotka in September 1989 on a Soviet ferryboat for a two-week visit with her relatives.

ALEXANDER "SASHA" BELAYEV. Sasha was born and raised in a small town near Moscow. Following six years of undergraduate studies at the Moscow Institute of Steel and

Alloys, he worked as engineer at aluminum smelting plants, including one in Krasnoyarsk, Siberia.

In 1987 he completed three years of graduate studies at the Moscow Institute and now holds a position there as a research assistant.

Sasha went on his first expedition—with Dmitry—in 1978 and has since been on nearly a dozen, including the Polar Ski Trek, which reached the North Pole in April 1988.

Following the Bering Bridge Expedition, Sasha received a three-month visa to visit Alaska, where he is working at the University's Center for International Business.

ALEXANDER TENYAKSHEV. Alexander told Paul that even as a child he was a whiz with anything electronic. Born and raised in Moscow, he holds a professorship at the Moscow Communications Institute. He has served as radio base operator for nearly all of Dmitry's expeditions, but the Bering Bridge Expedition was only the second time that he has been part of the trail team.

Using an ingenious series of interlocking ski poles and guy lines, he erected a 30-foot radio antenna tower nearly each day of the journey to help the team keep in touch with his Chukot-kan base as well as the American base in Nome.

ZOYA IVANOVA. Zoya was born in Naukan, an ancient Yupik village on the easternmost tip of the Soviet mainland. When the government relocated villagers to larger settlements nearby in the '50s, Zoya's family moved to Lavrentiya.

She attended medical school in Khabarovsk, a large city in southeast Siberia, and has since worked as a pediatrician in the Lavrentiya clinic. Her husband, Ivanov Yuri, is a Slavic Russian who holds a job as a government administrator.

Zoya is a lead drummer with her village's Eskimo dance company and practices with them several times a week.

VADIM KRIVOLAP. Vadim was born to a Chukchi mother, from whom he got his dark complexion and almond eyes, and Slavic Russian father, from whom he got his mop of curly black hair.

Following high school, he worked on a fishing boat. Later he became the director of Komsomol, the Youth Communist League, in his hometown of Neshkan, a village of 900 along the north coast of Chukotka. Vadim and his wife, Sveta, a Slavic Russian who works at the village's skin clothing workshop, have no children. Vadim, whose Chukchi name means "eternal light," is a skilled hunter and reindeer herder.

NICHOLAI "COLA" ATTINYA. Cola and Vadim have been best friends since childhood. Cola's father was a famous Chukchi hunter and dog handler who taught Cola the skills of life on the tundra and gave him his Eskimo name—"woman's knife." The knife is an essential tool in a culture that is entirely dependent on women for the preparation of all food and clothing.

A short, strapping bundle of muscle, Cola is a superb athlete and has achieved the distinction of Master Sport, one of the highest athletic honors awarded in the Soviet Union. He has competed in wrestling tournaments all over his country and serves as the school wrestling coach in Neshkan.

Cola maintains a kennel of sled dogs that are so well trained that he can fall asleep on his sled at the end of a day's hunt on the tundra, knowing his dogs will return him to his village.

EQUIPMENT AND SUPPLIES

8 purebred Canadian Eskimo freight dogs
11 mixed breed Soviet sled dogs
4 ten-foot aluminum and plastic freight sleds, based on
    Tim White's designs and marketed by Sawtooth
    Mountain sled works, Grand Marais, Minnesota
24 X-back freight harnesses by Rae's Harness Shop
Aircraft-cable gang lines and stake-out lines
    by Mark Nordman, Grand Marais, Minnesota
1,500 pounds Hills Pet Products Science Diet "Endurance"
    dog food
50 Polar Plus dog booties
3 Soviet six-person dome tents, aluminum top rings and
    inner and outer nylon shells
14 Caribou "Quasar" Quallofil sleeping bags
24 Ridge Rest Ensolite sleeping bags, Thermax and
    vapor-barrier sleeping bag liners
14 nylon bivy-sack sleeping bag shells
16 R.E.I. headlamps
16 pair Fischer "Europa 99" metal-edged back-country skis
Berwyn Zytel-nylon snow boot ski bindings
16 pair Excel Arctic fiberglass ski poles
12 R.E.I. "Northstar" internal frame backpacks
Swix ski waxes and ski scrapers
12 Carerra glacier sunglasses and ski goggles
"II Morrow" Loran "C" navigation unit
12 Brunton compasses
4 sets of Soviet and American topographic charts
6 Soviet pressurized white gas stoves
16 stainless steel Thermoses
14 stainless steel cups, bowls and spoons
3 aluminum cook pots
4 polyethelene fuel containers
24 hard-bound diaries, pens and pencils
200 rolls Kodachrome 36-64ASA slide film
16 U.S. and Soviet flags
Nikon FM2 35mm still camera

Sony 8-millimeter video camera

Bear rifles: AK-47s on Soviet side and Magnum 300 on U.S. side

Soviet emergency rubber life rafts

Emergency Medical Kit

2 SBX 11 SSB HF Transceivers

Soviet field radio

2 Emergency Locator Beacons

Flares

Custom-made ski boots by Red Wing Shoe Company of waterproof leather made by S.B. Foot Tanning Company, Red Wing, Minnesota

Servus Rubber's "Boundary by Northerner" super-insulated camp boots "Surefoot" neoprene boot insoles

Thermax liner socks

Thermax work socks

Hollofil work socks by Fox River

"Wintergreen" anorak Supplex nylon windshell parka and pants

"Wintergreen" Polar Plus insulating parka and pants

"Wintergreen" pile vest

Expedition-weight Thermax thermalwear tops and bottoms

"Wintergreen" extra heavy weight Thermax shirt

"Wintergreen" Cordura/Supplex overmitts

"Wintergreen" Polar Plus insulating mitten liners

Thermax ski gloves

"Wintergreen" wool wristlets

Neoprene face mask

Thermax balaclava face mask

Thermax ski hat

"Wintergreen" Polar Plus expedition hat

Complete set of Eskimo skin clothing including caribou parka and pants, sealskin boots and wolfskin hats